LADONNA NATURALE

The Business of Healthcare

Lining the Pockets of Pharmaceutical Companies,
Providers, and Politicians

OTIS
PUBLISHING

Contents

1

Introduction

In a brightly lit hospital room, after what seemed to be a routine appendectomy, John, a middle-aged school teacher, was handed a bill that nearly knocked the wind out of him. The total came to an astounding $30,000—a sum far exceeding his yearly budget for unexpected expenses, let alone medical bills. As he sifted through the pages, trying to make sense of the various charges, a sinking feeling of betrayal set in. How could a standard procedure result in such a financial burden? How many others were just like him, blindsided and feeling powerless against a system they barely understood?

This book is born out of a necessity to expose and untangle the intricate web that forms the business side of healthcare. In this sector, pharmaceutical companies, healthcare providers, and political interests intertwine more tightly than most of us realize. I aim to arm you, the reader, with the tools to confidently navigate this labyrinth and advocate for yourself in an ecosystem seemingly stacked against the average individual. It's about shifting the scales back into our favor, even if just slightly.

I come to you not just as an author but as someone who has navigated these murky waters both personally and professionally. My journey has been one of extensive research, countless interviews with insiders—doctors, nurses, policy experts—and experiences shared by patients who have all struggled within this system. These interactions have provided a solid foundation for the insights I offer, crafted to demystify the complexities of the healthcare industry for you.

This book is for every adult who has ever felt overwhelmed by the healthcare system. Whether you've faced exorbitant medical bills out of the blue or spent hours trying to decode your insurance coverage, this book is written for you. It doesn't matter if you're a healthcare professional looking for deeper insights or a layperson searching for guidance—this text is crafted to be accessible and engaging to all.

Structured into distinct parts, this book first explores the history and evolution of the healthcare industry. Then, it delves into the direct impacts on patients and the overarching influence of pharmaceutical and insurance sectors. It discusses potential solutions and a vision for a more equitable healthcare landscape. Each section builds upon the last, educating and empowering you to make informed decisions and advocate for change.

At the heart of this exploration is a simple yet powerful message: knowledge is power. I encourage you to approach this book not just as a collection of facts and narratives but as a vital tool for empowerment. With this knowledge, you can challenge opaque billing practices, demand more transparent communication from your providers, and consider healthier alternatives that pharmaceutical options might otherwise overshadow.

Let us begin this journey together with open minds and critical eyes. Use what you learn here to challenge the status quo, push for transparency, and advocate for a healthier, more patient-centric approach to healthcare.

Chapter 1 The Foundation of Modern Healthcare

In the late 19th century, a quiet revolution began in small, relatively inconspicuous laboratories. These humble beginnings marked the genesis of what we now call "Big Pharma"—a sector that has grown into a towering presence over the healthcare landscape. This chapter peels back the layers of pharmaceutical influence, revealing how, from these modest roots, an industry has risen to wield substantial power over healthcare practices, policy-making, and consumer behavior. As you embark on this exploration, consider not just the historical trajectory but the implications of such growth on your healthcare experiences and choices.

1.1 The Evolution of Pharmaceutical Influence

The Rise of Big Pharma

The transformation of pharmaceutical companies from niche chemical suppliers to global behemoths is a story of innovation, aggressive marketing, strategic regulation, and evolving public health needs. Initially focused on small-scale production of basic drugs, the industry experienced a boom with the discovery of penicillin in 1928. This event marked the beginning of antibiotics and opened floodgates to a new era of drug development. As these companies grew, so did their influence. The latter half of the 20th century saw a shift as pharmaceutical companies became the architects of their destiny—actively shaping healthcare agendas to fit their business models.

This growth trajectory was about more than just increased production capacities or revenue figures. It fundamentally altered the very fabric of healthcare. As these companies grew, they began to exert a disproportionate influence on what drugs were developed, how they were marketed, and, crucially, how they were incorporated into the standard medical practice. This pivot has sometimes aligned with the overarching goal of health care: to treat and heal. It has often been swayed by the prospects of profitability and market control, raising questions about aligning corporate gains with genuine healthcare needs.

Influence on Medical Practices

You might wonder how deep the roots of pharmaceutical influence run within everyday medical practices. The answer is far-reaching. The influence manifests in various forms, from the evident to the insidious. For instance, the prevalence of prescription drugs in modern treatment protocols must be considered. While many of these medications have undeniably

5

brought profound benefits, there's an underlying narrative of over-prescription influenced by pharmaceutical marketing rather than patient necessity. This scenario often leads to a cascade of effects, from side effects requiring further medication to the rampant issue of antibiotic resistance spurred by overuse.

Moreover, pharmaceutical companies have mastered the art of 'disease mongering'—a practice where conditions are marketed alongside the drugs meant to treat them, expanding the market under the guise of spreading awareness. This tactic not only skews public perception but also nudges medical practices towards a more pharmaceutical-dependent model of care.

Lobbying Power

Pharmaceutical lobbying is a powerhouse with deep pockets and wide-reaching influence, spending billions annually to sway laws, policies, and regulations in its favor. The implications of this lobbying power are profound and multifaceted, affecting everything from drug pricing to the approval processes of new medications. Through lobbying, pharmaceutical companies can shape healthcare policies, prioritizing market needs over public health. This reality is evident in the extended patent lives of drugs, which keep prices high by delaying the entry of cheaper generics, making healthcare less affordable for you and millions of others.

Direct-to-Consumer Marketing

Turning on your television or browsing the internet, you will likely encounter direct-to-consumer (DTC) pharmaceutical advertisements—flashing catchy slogans, heartwarming scenes, and simplified lists of potential side effects. The United States and New Zealand stand out globally for allowing such practices. The influence of DTC marketing is significant, empowering pharmaceutical companies to communicate directly with you, the consumer, potentially bypassing the filter provided by healthcare professionals. This form of marketing impacts patient treatment choices and significantly escalates healthcare costs. It creates a demand for newer, often more expensive drugs, which may not necessarily offer improved outcomes over existing, less costly alternatives.

The narrative of pharmaceutical influence in healthcare is complex and multifaceted, woven deeply into the fabric of medical practices, policy-making, and consumer behavior. As this chapter unfolds, it invites you to reflect on these dynamics— not just as abstract concepts but as realities that affect your health, choices, and financial well-being.

1.2 Insurance Dynamics: A Double-Edged Sword

The narrative of health insurance in the United States is a tale of evolution, from a rudimentary form of coverage in the early 20th century to an intricate system enabling and complicating access to healthcare today. Initially, health insurance was designed to help individuals manage financial risks associated with unpre-dictable medical costs, particularly during the Great Depression. However, its purpose and structure have shifted significantly over the decades. Due to wage controls and tax incentives, the

7

advent of employer-sponsored health insurance during World War II marked a pivotal shift, embedding insurance deeply into the American healthcare landscape. This growth was not just an expansion in numbers but also an increase in the complexity of the insurance models and their impact on healthcare access and delivery.

The transformation of health insurance has had profound implications for healthcare costs. As the intermediary between healthcare providers and patients, insurance companies wield considerable power in determining the pricing structures within healthcare. The role of insurance should naturally lead to cost control. However, the reality is often the opposite. The presence of insurance sometimes artificially inflates the demand for healthcare services, as providers may extend more services than necessary, knowing that the costs are buffered by insurance coverage. This phenomenon, known as the moral hazard, complicates the pricing dynamics significantly. Moreover, the administrative costs associated with managing healthcare plans—everything from processing claims to marketing and managing fraud—are substantial and contribute directly to the rising cost of healthcare. These overhead expenses, necessary for the functioning of insurance companies, ultimately trickle down to policyholders in the form of higher premiums.

Equally significant is how insurance design can prevent access to necessary medical care. High premiums, daunting deductibles, and substantial copayments can deter individuals from seeking timely medical interventions, leading to worse health outcomes and, paradoxically, higher overall healthcare costs due to the need for more intensive treatments at later stages. For instance, consider a scenario where a person with a high-deductible health plan delays visiting a healthcare provider for symptoms of what is later diagnosed as diabetes. The initial cost-saving from not visiting the doctor is vastly overshadowed by the long-term expenses of treating advanced diabetes, which could have been mitigated with earlier intervention. This barrier is not merely financial but psychological, as the fear of unexpected bills can discourage even insured individuals from engaging with the healthcare system until necessary.

The inherent conflict of interest between insurance company profits and the provision of patient care is one of the most contentious issues within the healthcare system. Insurance companies, as businesses, inherently aim to maximize profit and shareholder value. This goal can sometimes lead to practices that conflict with the optimal care of patients. For instance, the practice of denying coverage for specific treatments or drugs as a cost-saving measure can directly contradict the medical needs of patients. Similarly, the lengthy and convoluted process of claims approvals can delay necessary treatments, compromising patient health in the name of procedural compliance. This misalignment of priorities—profit over patient care— underscores a fundamental tension in the role of insurance in healthcare, questioning whether the current models adequately fulfill their intended role of facilitating access to healthcare.

Navigating this landscape requires a nuanced understanding of health insurance's history and mechanics—it is not simply a financial tool but a determinant of healthcare quality and accessibility. As such, the dynamics of health insurance remain a double-edged sword, capable of enabling and hindering millions' health outcomes. As we explore these complexities, it becomes clear that any efforts to reform healthcare must address the pivotal role of insurance with a critical eye and innovative thinking, aiming to realign the system to serve the populace's health better.

1.3 The Political Chessboard of Healthcare

Understanding the political landscape of healthcare requires peering behind the curtain to see how deeply entrenched interests shape the game's rules, often at the expense of public health priorities. The interplay between healthcare lobbying, campaign financing, and regulatory capture creates a complex web that often perpetuates the status quo and resists fundamental changes that could benefit the broader population. This exploration into the political underpinnings of healthcare reveals how significant decisions that affect millions are often swayed by a select few.

Healthcare lobbying is a formidable force in shaping legislation and policy at both federal and state levels. Pharmaceutical companies and insurance providers deploy armies of lobbyists whose job is to ensure that the interests of these corporations are well-represented in the halls of power. The influence is profound and multifaceted, impacting everything from healthcare legislation's specifics to healthcare policy's broader orientation. For instance, lobbyists work tirelessly to block or dilute legislative efforts to cap drug prices or bring more transparency to insurance practices. This relentless lobbying perpetuates a system where policy decisions often tilt favorably towards industry giants rather than focusing on improving accessibility and affordability for you and your family. The impact is not just in the legislation passed but also in the potential reforms stymied before they ever reach a vote.

Campaign financing further entangles the healthcare industry with the political sphere. Healthcare corporations invest heavily in political campaigns, ensuring they have a seat at the table in policy discussions. This investment creates an environment where politicians, consciously or not, may prioritize their major donors' interests over their constituents' needs. The quid pro quo nature of this relationship is rarely overt. Still, it can be discerned in the reluctance of lawmakers to support bills that might contradict the interests of their major donors from the healthcare sector. This dynamic is troubling not only because it undermines the democratic process but also because it has tangible effects on the healthcare policies that shape everyday lives. It raises the cost of healthcare and limits the scope of available medical services, making it increasingly difficult for the average citizen to afford and access necessary care.

Regulatory capture is one of the most insidious ways the health-care industry exerts influence. This phenomenon occurs when regulatory agencies, created to act in the public interest, come to be dominated by the industries they are supposed to regulate. Through various mechanisms—such as the revolving door between regulatory agencies and the healthcare industry, where individuals routinely switch roles as industry advocates and regulators—these agencies often become more responsive to industry desires than public needs. This shift can lead to lax oversight, weak enforcement of regulations, and a tendency to prioritize industry profitability over public health outcomes. The consequences are far-reaching, affecting drug safety, the efficacy of medical treatments, and the overall integrity of our healthcare system.

The battles over healthcare reform provide a clear lens through which to view these dynamics. Critical legislative efforts, such as the Affordable Care Act, have been battlegrounds of political ideologies and industry influence. Lobbying efforts by insurance and pharmaceutical companies have shaped these reforms profoundly, often diluting their effectiveness to protect industry profits. The tug-of-war in Congress over such reforms is a stark reminder of private interests' power in public policy-making. These battles are not just political theater—they represent conflicts over who benefits from how healthcare is administered in this country, with high stakes for all involved.

As these elements coalesce, the political landscape of healthcare often seems designed more to sustain industry profits than to improve health outcomes or reduce patient costs. This realization is not just a critique; it's a call to reevaluate how health policies are made and whose interests they truly serve. By understanding the forces at play, citizens and policymakers can begin to advocate for a system that places the populace's well-being at its heart, challenging the entrenched powers that have shaped healthcare to its current form.

3

Chapter 2 The Players and Their Playgrounds

As we peel back the layers of the healthcare industry's business practices, it becomes crucial to scrutinize the roles and strategies of the key players within this complex ecosystem. Among these, pharmaceutical companies, or Big Pharma, stand out due to their profound impact on healthcare dynamics. This chapter delves into the multifaceted influence of these corporations, exploring how their marketing strategies, lobbying efforts, patent manipulations, and research priorities shape the landscape of global healthcare. By understanding these tactics, you can better navigate the healthcare system, advocate for change, and make informed decisions about your health.

2.1 Big Pharma's Grip on Healthcare

Marketing Tactics

The aggressive marketing tactics employed by pharmaceutical companies are not just about selling drugs; they are about creating a culture where medication is often seen as the first and sometimes only option for managing health issues. These tactics manifest through several channels, each tailored to maximize impact and drive sales. For instance, consider the ubiquitous drug ads that not only populate your TV screens and web pages but also appear in the waiting rooms of your local clinics. These ads, often featuring compelling narratives of recovery and rejuvenation, are designed to create a direct appeal to you, bypassing healthcare professionals.

Moreover, pharmaceutical representatives play a crucial role in these marketing strategies. Armed with persuasive pitches and often substantial budgets for free samples and sponsored lunches, these representatives visit doctors' offices to convince healthcare providers to prescribe their drugs. This face-to-face marketing is highly effective, influencing prescribing habits through personal charm and professional persistence. However, the ethical implications of such interactions are significant, raising questions about the influence of commercial interests on medical decisions that should prioritize patient health above all.

Lobbying Efforts

Pharmaceutical companies invest heavily in lobbying, ensuring their interests are well-represented in power. The scope of this lobbying is vast, encompassing efforts to sway drug pricing policies, influence new healthcare regulations, and shape the patent laws that protect their products. In the United States alone, the pharmaceutical and health product industry spends billions of dollars on lobbying annually, making it one of the top spenders in the lobbying arena. This financial power translates into significant political influence, affecting every facet of healthcare policy—from the approval of new drugs to the pricing mechanisms that determine their cost to you.

This extensive lobbying creates a healthcare landscape where policies often favor the profitability of pharmaceutical companies, sometimes at the expense of patient access to affordable medications. For example, lobbying efforts can delay the introduction of generic drugs, which are typically cheaper than their brand-name counterparts. By influencing legislation and regulatory practices, Big Pharma succeeds in maintaining high drug prices and controlling the market, a practice that directly impacts your medical expenses and access to necessary treatments.

Patent Manipulation

One of the most critical areas in which pharmaceutical companies exert influence is managing drug patents. Patents protect intellectual property, granting companies a temporary monopoly on their products to recoup research and development investments. However, the strategic manipulation of these patents, often called "evergreening," involves making minor changes to a drug—such as altering its dosage form or combining it with another drug—to extend its patent protection and keep generics off the market.

This manipulation blocks the entry of cheaper, generic alternatives, maintaining high drug prices and limiting your access to affordable medication options. The consequences of these actions are far-reaching, affecting not only individual healthcare costs but also the overall sustainability of healthcare systems. As patents prevent generic competition, they stifle innovation and maintain a status quo where older, less effective drugs remain predominant because they are more profitable.

Impact on Research and Development

The priorities of pharmaceutical companies significantly influence the direction of research and development (R&D) in the healthcare field. While one might assume that R&D would be guided by the pressing health needs of the population, the reality is often more complex and driven by market considerations. For example, there is a notable trend towards developing "lifestyle drugs" that target chronic, non-life-threatening conditions, which are more profitable because they command a lifelong market.

Moreover, the focus on developing drugs that are only marginally better than existing ones rather than breakthrough therapies is symptomatic of an R&D strategy driven by profit motives rather than genuine healthcare innovation. This approach results in significant resources allocated to developing drugs that offer minimal therapeutic advances, overlooking less profitable but more urgently needed medical treatments. This misalignment between R&D priorities and public health needs underscores the profound impact of pharmaceutical companies' strategies on the trajectory of global healthcare development.

As we continue to explore the intricate relationships and practices within the healthcare industry, it becomes increasingly
clear that Big Pharma's influence is a pivotal factor in shaping
the healthcare experience for individuals around the world.
Understanding these dynamics is not just about critiquing the
status quo; it is about empowering you to make informed choices
and advocate for a healthcare system prioritizing human health
over corporate profits.

2.2 Healthcare Providers: Between a Rock and a Hard Place

Healthcare providers operate in an increasingly complex environment, squeezed by financial pressures from various fronts
and ethical dilemmas that challenge the very heart of their professional commitments. One of the most significant financial
pressures comes from insurance reimbursements, often fraught
with delays, denials, and demands for excessive documentation.
For many healthcare providers, these reimbursement rates must
catch up with the rising medical practice costs. This includes
everything from leasing office space to purchasing the latest
medical technology. Coupled with the intensifying costs of
pharmaceuticals, particularly the high prices of specialty drugs,
the financial landscape for many practitioners needs to be more
sustainable. This squeeze affects the stability of their practices
and their ability to provide care. When reimbursements are
adequate, providers may be able to see more patients in less
time or make difficult decisions about which services they can
afford to offer, potentially compromising the quality of care
they can provide.

Furthermore, the ethical dilemmas that healthcare providers face are manifold and profound. On one hand, they entered the profession to deliver the best possible care and prioritize their patients' well-being. On the other, they find themselves navigating a healthcare system that often seems more concerned with bottom lines than patient outcomes. This dichotomy can lead to significant stress and moral distress among providers. For example, physicians might feel compelled to prescribe a medication not because it is the best choice for the patient but because it is the only option covered under the patient's insurance plan.

Similarly, the rising influence of pharmaceutical companies can skew prescribing practices. Armed with persuasive data and sometimes incentives, sales representatives can sway doctors towards newer, more expensive medications that may not necessarily offer improved outcomes over older, less costly alternatives. This influence can subtly shift treatment plans away from the ideal standards of care, nudging healthcare providers into ethical gray areas where the patient's best interest may not always be the clear guiding principle.

Adapting to ongoing healthcare reforms adds another layer of complexity for providers. Over the past decades, numerous changes have been aimed at improving the efficiency, cost-effectiveness, and quality of healthcare. For instance, the shift towards value-based care models, where providers are reimbursed based on patient health outcomes rather than the volume of care delivered, aims to align healthcare practices with healthier long-term patient outcomes. While the principles behind such reforms are commendable, implementing them can be a formidable challenge. Many providers must overhaul their practice's infrastructure, invest in new technology to track compliance and outcomes, and retrain staff to meet different operational demands. While potentially beneficial in the long run, these changes require significant upfront investments of time and resources, often without immediate financial benefits. This transition period can be particularly strenuous, testing the resilience and adaptability of providers who must keep up with the reforms while delivering day-to-day patient care.

The landscape in which healthcare providers operate today is one of tremendous pressure and change, requiring a careful balancing act between financial sustainability, ethical integrity, and the demands of an evolving healthcare system. As they navigate these challenges, providers must continuously maintain their commitment to patient care despite the constraints and influences that may pull them in opposite directions. The ability to adapt, uphold ethical standards, and manage financial pressures is crucial for their practices and fundamental to the health of the communities they serve. Understanding these pressures and dilemmas is essential for anyone looking to navigate, reform, or understand the healthcare landscape more deeply.

2.3 Regulatory Bodies: Gatekeepers or Facilitators?

Regulatory bodies such as the Food and Drug Administration (FDA) in the United States are pivotal in maintaining the safety and efficacy of drugs and treatments that reach the market.

As gatekeepers, these organizations are tasked with a critical balancing act: ensuring that new medical products are safe for public use and made available promptly to those who need them. The approval process involves rigorous scientific evaluation and testing to verify that the benefits of a drug or treatment outweigh its risks. This process is vital in preventing the recurrence of past healthcare disasters where unsafe drugs caused significant harm before being detected by regulators. As part of their role in safeguarding public health, regulatory bodies also monitor drugs' ongoing safety post-approval, allowing them to react swiftly if unforeseen issues arise once the product is used in the broader population.

Despite their crucial role, these regulatory bodies face numerous challenges that can impede their ability to protect public health effectively. One major challenge is the pace of pharmaceutical development, which has accelerated with advances in science and technology. As new classes of drugs and complex biologics enter the market, regulators must constantly update their skills and knowledge to keep pace. This rapid development can strain the resources of regulatory agencies, leading to backlogs and delays that can, paradoxically, slow the availability of lifesaving treatments. Additionally, the marketing strategies employed by pharmaceutical companies have grown increasingly sophisti- cated, utilizing digital platforms and targeted campaigns that can blur the lines between educational content and promotional material. This evolution requires constant vigilance from regulatory bodies to ensure that marketing practices do not mislead consumers or healthcare providers about the risks and benefits of drugs.

Conflicts of interest present another significant challenge for regulatory bodies. The intersection of public health goals with the profit-driven motives of the pharmaceutical industry can lead to situations where the impartiality of regulatory decisions is called into question. For instance, hiring industry experts with previous ties to pharmaceutical companies can lead to potential biases in drug approval processes. Furthermore, the funding of regulatory agencies often involves fees paid by the very companies seeking product approval, which could be perceived as a conflict of interest. These relationships necessitate stringent policies to maintain the integrity of regulatory decisions, ensuring that they are based solely on scientific evidence and public health needs, not on industry influences.

Increased transparency and accountability in the regulatory process are paramount in maintaining public trust. Transparency initiatives, such as the public disclosure of clinical trial data and the basis for regulatory decisions, help demystify the process and allow independent experts and the public to scrutinize the findings. This openness helps reassure the public that regulatory actions are taken in their best interests, free from undue industry influence. Accountability measures, including regular audits and the possibility of sanctions for regulatory failures, ensure that these bodies adhere to high standards of conduct and rectify mistakes swiftly. These steps are essential in fostering a regulatory environment where public health priorities are precise and paramount, reinforcing the role of regulatory bodies as protectors and facilitators of health and safety.

As we reflect on the complexities of the regulatory landscape in healthcare, it's clear that these bodies face a delicate task. They must navigate the pressures of rapid pharmaceutical innovation, complex marketing tactics, and potential internal conflicts of interest, all while maintaining the trust of the public whose health they are charged to protect. The effectiveness of regulatory bodies in fulfilling their roles impacts the immediate safety of medical treatments and shapes the broader public confidence in the healthcare system as a whole.

In summary, the challenges faced by regulatory bodies are significant and multifaceted. Their success in overcoming these challenges is crucial for ensuring that the healthcare products reaching the market are safe and effective. As we transition to the next chapter, we will explore the hidden mechanisms of the healthcare industry, shedding light on less visible but equally impactful aspects of healthcare, such as the intricacies of clinical trials and the complexities of drug pricing. This continued exploration will further demystify the forces shaping our healthcare experiences and empower us with the knowledge to advocate for a system that genuinely prioritizes health and well-being.

4

Chapter 3 The Hidden Mechanisms

Beneath the surface of the healthcare industry's bustling activity lies a less visible but profoundly influential layer, the realm of clinical trials. These trials, the bedrock upon which medical safety and efficacy standards are built, are often shrouded in practices that may not always align with the transparent, altruistic ideals we hold. As we delve deeper into this critical phase of drug development, it becomes essential to peel back the layers to understand not just the outcomes but the processes and practices that may affect the integrity of the healthcare treatments you rely on.

3.1 The Secret Life of Clinical Trials

Clinical trials are the cornerstone of medical progress, providing the data necessary to evaluate new treatments. However, the integrity of these trials can be compromised by the selective publication of data, a practice that may cast long shadows over their reliability. Imagine, if you will, a scenario where only favorable outcomes of a drug trial are reported while those results that show no effect or adverse outcomes are withheld. This selective reporting can skew a treatment's perceived efficacy and safety, influencing medical professionals' prescribing habits and patient choices. The implications are profound, as treatment decisions based on incomplete data may be ineffective and potentially harmful.

The accessibility of clinical trial data is another area of concern. In an ideal world, all data from clinical trials would be readily available to researchers and practitioners, allowing for independent verification of results and fostering an environment of open scientific inquiry. However, the reality often needs to catch up to this ideal. This data remains inaccessible, locked behind the walls of proprietary interests, or unpublished due to unfavorable outcomes. This lack of transparency hinders the advancement of medical science and practice, as it prevents the whole body of knowledge from being openly reviewed and integrated into the broader medical understanding.

Influence on Medical Guidelines

The data from clinical trials plays a crucial role in shaping medical guidelines and guiding the treatment protocols used across healthcare systems. However, when the pharmaceutical industry's interests influence clinical trials, these guidelines might only sometimes be built on an unbiased foundation. It is not uncommon for trials to be designed in ways that favor the drug being tested—by selecting specific patient demographics or comparing them with less effective treatments. Such designs can lead to guidelines recommending new, more expensive medications without clear evidence of their superiority over existing, often less costly alternatives. This practice has implications for healthcare costs and impacts the quality of care you receive, potentially steering treatment away from more effective, established options.

Patient Recruitment and Consent

The ethical considerations in patient recruitment and informed consent are paramount. Patients must be fully informed of the risks and benefits of participating in a trial, a process that should be free of coercion and misunderstanding. However, the recruitment process can sometimes be influenced by the urgent need to meet enrollment numbers, leading to patients not being fully informed or feeling pressured to participate. Moreover, the complexity of clinical trial information can be daunting, and without adequate explanation, patients might consent to participation without fully understanding the implications. Ensuring that consent is genuinely informed requires a meticulous, patient-centric approach that respects each participant's autonomy and right to make an informed decision about their involvement in research that could affect their health profoundly.

In this complex interplay of data manipulation, access limitations, influence on medical standards, and ethical recruitment practices, the narrative of clinical trials is one of nuanced challenges. It underscores the need for vigilance, transparency, and moral rigor to ensure that these trials serve their fundamental purpose—to advance medical knowledge and improve patient care reliably and ethically. As we continue to explore the hidden mechanisms of the healthcare industry, remember that each layer we uncover adds to our understanding, empowering us to advocate for a system that upholds the highest standards of integrity and care.

3.2 The Pricing Puzzle: Decoding Drug Costs

The relationship between the costs of drugs and their value to patients and the healthcare system is a tapestry woven with numerous threads, each representing different financial, ethical, and health-related concerns. When evaluating a medication, one might consider its effectiveness in treating a condition, but an equally important aspect is its cost relative to its therapeutic benefits. This cost-value relationship is critical, as it impacts not only individual health outcomes but also the broader economics of healthcare systems. For instance, a drug might offer a marginal improvement over existing treatments but at a significantly higher cost. Here, the question arises: do the additional benefits justify the extra expense? This question becomes particularly poignant in scenarios involving lifesaving medications, where the price tags can soar into the thousands, placing immense financial burdens on patients and insurance systems alike. These scenarios underscore the need for a critical assessment of drug pricing, ensuring that prices are justified by genuine therapeutic advancements rather than artificially inflated by market dynamics or monopolistic practices.

The opacity of drug pricing strategies further complicates this landscape. Pharmaceutical companies often set drug prices that do not transparently correlate with research and development or production costs. Instead, these prices are frequently influenced by what the market will bear, leading to significant disparities in what is charged for the same medication in different contexts or regions. The need for more transparency in pricing is a deliberate strategy for many companies, as it prevents a precise analysis of pricing fairness and impedes efforts to regulate drug costs effectively. This strategy affects affordability and raises ethical questions about profit-making in life-critical sectors. For you and many others, this lack of clarity in drug pricing can be frustrating and disheartening, especially when faced with high medical bills that are difficult to justify.

Pharmacy benefit managers (PBMs) play a significant role in the drug pricing ecosystem, acting as intermediaries between pharmaceutical companies and healthcare payers, such as insurance companies and pharmacies. While PBMs are tasked with negotiating lower drug prices on behalf of insurers, their role has become controversial due to practices that may only sometimes align with the interests of patients. For example, PBMs often receive rebates from pharmaceutical companies for favoring higher-priced drugs on their formularies, which are lists of drugs that insurance plans agree to cover. This practice can create a conflict of interest, where PBMs might prioritize drugs that bring them higher rebates than those most cost-effective for patients. As a result, these middlemen can contribute to higher overall healthcare costs, complicating efforts to make medications affordable for you and others who depend on these drugs for quality of life.

When examining drug prices internationally, stark discrepancies become evident. The same medication can often be purchased in other countries at a fraction of the cost charged in the U.S. These differences are mainly due to various countries' healthcare and pharmaceutical regulation approaches. For instance, many countries with national health systems have government entities that negotiate drug prices directly with pharmaceutical companies, resulting in lower prices. In contrast, the U.S. relies on a more market-driven approach, where multiple payers negotiate separately with pharmaceutical companies, often resulting in higher prices. Understanding these international pricing discrepancies is crucial, as it highlights alternative pharmaceutical regulation approaches that could lead to more equitable pricing. By looking at these models, you can gain insights into how systemic changes might be implemented domestically to address the high costs of medications, thus ensuring that essential drugs are accessible to all who need them.

Exploring the complexities of drug costs and their justifications reveals a convoluted picture where ethical, economic, and health-related factors intersect. This exploration illuminates the challenges of ensuring fair pricing in the pharmaceutical industry and highlights the broader implications of these costs for public health and equity. As you navigate your healthcare needs and choices, understanding these dynamics can empower you to advocate for more transparent and fair drug pricing, ultimately aiming for a healthcare system prioritizing human well-being over profit.

3.3 Patent Wars and Generic Drugs

The intricate dance between patent protection and generic drug production is a critical aspect of pharmaceutical economics that significantly impacts healthcare costs and accessibility. Patent cliffs represent a pivotal moment when a brand-name drug's patent expires, allowing generic manufacturers to produce cheaper versions of the drug. This transition can dramatically reduce costs and broaden access to medication. However, pharmaceutical companies often employ strategic legal maneuvers to extend their patents—a practice known as "evergreening." These extensions can involve slight modifications to the formulation of a drug or its delivery mechanism, which, while legally justifiable, may offer minimal clinical improvement over the original. This tactic is a double-edged sword: it protects the financial investments into drug development and delays affordable generics' availability.

The implications of these patent wars extend deeply into the generic drug market, affecting both availability and cost. When patents are extended, generic manufacturers are blocked or delayed from entering the market with cheaper alternatives. This delay means that patients and healthcare systems continue to pay higher prices for brand-name drugs. For many, especially those without substantial insurance coverage, these costs can make essential medications financially out of reach, leading to gaps in treatment and worse health outcomes. Moreover, the uncertainty around patent expirations can stifle competition, as generic manufacturers may hesitate to invest in the production of a drug if they fear unexpected patent extensions will undermine their market entry.

The legal battles fought over pharmaceutical patents raise significant ethical considerations. On the one hand, the protection provided by patents is fundamental to recouping the investments made in drug research and development, potentially fostering innovation by ensuring companies can profit from their inventions. On the other hand, these protections can become barriers to access, particularly when used to artificially prolong the exclusivity of drug formulas whose actual therapeutic novelty is debatable. This tension poses a moral dilemma: balancing rewarding pharmaceutical innovation while ensuring essential medications are affordable and accessible to those in need.

Several high-profile case studies highlight these issues vividly. One notable example involves a leading pharmaceutical company that slightly modifies a popular medication used to treat a common chronic condition. The company could extend its patent for several years by altering the drug's release mechanism. Another case involved a company that engaged in a practice known as "pay-for-delay," where they paid a generic manufacturer to postpone the release of a cheaper version of a medication used by millions. These cases often end up in court, drawing public and professional scrutiny, and have prompted calls for reforms in patent law to better align with public health interests.

As we conclude this exploration of patent wars and their impact on the generic drug market, it is clear that the strategies employed by pharmaceutical companies to extend patents are deeply intertwined with broader issues of healthcare afford-ability and access. These practices, while legally permissible, often challenge our ethical standards and call for a careful consideration of how best to balance innovation with public health needs. This discussion sets the stage for the subsequent chapters, which will dive deeper into the solutions and reforms needed to address these complex challenges, aiming to foster a healthcare system that truly prioritizes patient care over profit.

5

Chapter 4 Patient Stories and Struggles

In the labyrinth of healthcare, where corridors of power weave through the lives of millions, personal stories illuminate the human side of statistics and policies. These narratives, filled with challenges, triumphs, and relentless struggles, bring a poignant clarity to the abstract complexities of the healthcare system. Each story is a unique thread in the broader tapestry of patient experiences, revealing the varied impacts of chronic illnesses, the hurdles in accessing mental health care, and the extraordinary resilience some display in navigating this daunting maze.

4.1 Voices from the Maze: Patient Experiences

Diverse Perspectives

The healthcare system, a behemoth of institutions, regulations, and practices, touches lives in profoundly different ways. Consider the story of Maria, a single mother battling breast cancer while juggling her job as a high school teacher. Her narrative sheds light on the emotional and physical toll of managing a chronic illness under the pressure of maintaining a stable family environment and professional responsibilities. Then there's Michael, a veteran who grapples with PTSD, navigating a maze of VA hospitals and community clinics, often finding himself lost in a sea of appointments and medications. These stories, and countless others like them, emphasize the spectrum of challenges faced by patients. Each narrative underscores the necessity for a healthcare system that is efficient, equitable, compassionate, and responsive to the diverse needs of its patients.

Impact of Chronic Illness

Living with a chronic illness often means navigating a perpetual storm and managing symptoms and treatments while trying to maintain some semblance of normalcy. Sarah, for example, lives with multiple sclerosis, a condition that presents not just a physical battle but an administrative one as well, as she coordinates care across multiple specialists and manages the side effects of numerous medications. Her days are punctuated by battles for insurance approvals and hours spent in waiting rooms, all while dealing with the fatigue and pain that are her constant companions. The energy and persistence required to manage a chronic illness can be overwhelming, making the importance of supportive care and streamlined healthcare processes clear. These are not just conveniences; they are lifelines for those already fighting daily to maintain their health and well-being.

Mental Health Journeys

The path to accessing mental health care is fraught with obstacles, from stigma to inadequate insurance coverage. Take the case of Jonah, a college student who struggled with depression for years before seeking help. His journey was hindered by a pervasive stigma around mental health in his community, where such issues were often dismissed or misunderstood. Once he decided to seek help, Jonah faced another hurdle: finding affordable therapy. His story highlights the critical gaps in our healthcare system that can delay or prevent access to necessary mental health services. These narratives underscore the need for a healthcare landscape that eradicates stigma and provides robust mental health support, recognizing that mental wellness is as crucial as physical health.

Success and Resilience

Despite the myriad challenges, there are stories of remarkable resilience and success—tales that offer hope and potential pathways for others. Linda, diagnosed with type 2 diabetes, managed to turn her prognosis around through a combination of diligent self-care, informed dietary choices, and regular physical activity. Her journey was supported by a healthcare provider who took the time to educate her about her condition and treatment options, empowering her to take control of her health. Linda's story is a testament to the power of patient education and the profound impact of proactive, compassionate healthcare providers who do more than treat symptoms—they educate and empower their patients.

Each of these stories brings to light the personal realities hidden behind the healthcare system's impersonal facade. They remind us that behind every policy decision, every medical bill, and every insurance form are individuals whose lives are profoundly affected by how effectively and empathetically we deliver healthcare. As we move forward, let these voices guide our efforts and inform our decisions, ensuring we always keep sight of the real human element at the heart of healthcare.

4.2 The High Cost of Living: Financial Burdens

The financial implications of healthcare extend far beyond the direct costs of treatment and medications; they seep into every facet of a patient's life, often with far-reaching consequences. Consider the scenario where out-of-pocket expenses accumulate from the expected costs of chronic disease management and the unpredictable expenses tied to emergency medical interventions. These costs can quickly deplete savings, strain credit, and push budgets to breaking points. Patients frequently face the daunting task of choosing between purchasing necessary medications and covering basic living expenses. This financial strain is not merely about numbers on a bill; it's about the stress and anxiety that come with financial instability, which can exacerbate health issues, creating a vicious cycle of health problems and financial woes.

Out-of-pocket expenses are particularly burdensome for individuals with high-deductible health plans. These plans, while offering lower monthly premiums, require a substantial amount of money to be paid out before insurance coverage fully kicks in. For many, this means that routine healthcare and necessary medications can become financially out of reach. The impact is stark, with patients often having to make painful decisions about delaying or skipping treatments, which can lead to severe health deterioration over time. The ripple effects are profound, affecting not just the physical health of individuals but their mental well-being and overall quality of life.

Insurance challenges add another layer of complexity to the financial trials patients face. Dealing with insurance can often feel like navigating a minefield of denied claims, endless paperwork, and frustrating bureaucratic hurdles. Patients find themselves in a constant battle to prove the necessity of treatments or to appeal unjust denials, which not only consumes their time but also adds to their stress and anxiety. High premiums and deductibles are only the tip of the iceberg. The real challenge lies in the unpredictability and opacity of insurance coverage, where patients often need clarification about what is covered once they receive a bill. This uncertainty can deter individuals from seeking necessary care in the first place, fearing the financial implications more than the medical consequences.

Medical debt is perhaps one of the most crippling financial burdens that can afflict anyone. It is a significant issue in the U.S., where medical expenses account for most personal bankruptcies. The path to medical debt is often swift and unexpected; a sudden health crisis can generate substantial medical bills that insurance may not fully cover, pushing individuals and families into financial peril. The consequences of medical debt extend beyond just financial health; they impact credit scores, which can affect a person's ability to buy a home, secure loans, or sometimes even find employment. The stigma and stress associated with medical debt can lead to significant mental health declines as individuals grapple with the dual burdens of debt and disease.

Cost-related non-adherence to prescribed treatments or medications directly results from these financial burdens. When faced with high costs, many patients choose to skip doses, split pills, or abandon treatment altogether. This form of non-adherence is not about forgetfulness or negligence; it's a survival strategy in the face of overwhelming financial pressure. However, the consequences of such decisions are dire. Non-adherence can lead to worsening medical conditions, increased hospitalizations, and higher overall healthcare costs in the long run. The irony is stark: in trying to save money in the short term, patients often end up facing even higher medical expenses down the road.

As we explore the layers of financial strain imposed by the healthcare system, it becomes clear that the costs involved in medical care are not just numbers on a bill. They represent barriers to wellness, catalysts for stress, and triggers for potentially life-altering financial crises. Understanding these financial dynamics is crucial for anyone navigating the healthcare system, as it underscores the need for more transparent, fair, and supportive financial structures within healthcare to truly support the well-being of patients.

4.3 Access Denied: The Barriers to Care

In exploring the healthcare landscape, it becomes evident that access to necessary medical services is not merely a matter of demand and supply but is significantly influenced by various deep-seated structural issues. Among these, geographic limitations are a formidable barrier to accessing quality healthcare. Individuals residing in rural or remote areas often need more medical facilities and healthcare professionals, which can delay diagnosis and limit treatment options. Such geographic disparities are not limited to sparse rural landscapes but are also prevalent in underserved urban neighborhoods where clinics might be overcrowded or underfunded. The lack of local, accessible medical services forces residents in these areas to travel long distances for care, which is not just inconvenient but often results in delayed or foregone treatment, exacerbating health conditions that could have been managed more effectively with timely intervention.

Furthermore, the gaps in insurance coverage represent another critical barrier to accessing healthcare. Despite various health reforms intended to increase coverage, many individuals find themselves in a coverage gap, not qualifying for Medicaid while also being unable to afford private insurance. Even those with insurance might discover that their plans do not cover certain necessary treatments or medications or that the financial costs associated with their plans' deductibles and co-pays are prohibitively expensive. These gaps are particularly acute in the case of mental health services and specialty care, which are frequently less covered than other types of healthcare. This lack of comprehensive coverage leaves many without essential healthcare services, forcing them to live with conditions that could otherwise be managed or cured, ultimately placing a more significant burden on the healthcare system through emergency room visits and serious health complications that could have been avoided.

The systemic inequalities that permeate our society also play a significant role in healthcare accessibility. Socioeconomic status, race, and ethnicity significantly influence an individual's ability to receive adequate healthcare. Studies consistently demonstrate that minority groups and economically disadvantaged communities face higher rates of chronic illness and lower rates of access to adequate healthcare. These inequalities are rooted in a complex mix of economic disparity, social determinants of health, and, at times, institutional biases within the healthcare system itself. Such disparities undermine the efforts to achieve equitable healthcare access and erode these communities' trust and engagement with the healthcare system.

Navigating the bureaucratic labyrinth of the healthcare system poses yet another hurdle. The complexity of insurance paperwork, the arduous process of securing referrals for specialist care, and the often opaque criteria for treatment approval can be daunting for many patients. This bureaucratic maze not only consumes time and resources but also adds a layer of stress and uncertainty to the patient experience. For those who are not adept at managing such complexities, particularly the elderly, those with lower educational attainment, or non-native language speakers, the bureaucracy can become an insurmountable barrier, preventing them from accessing the care they need and are entitled to receive.

The cumulative impact of these barriers—geographic, insurance-related, systemic, and bureaucratic—creates a healthcare environment where access is uneven and often aligned with factors other than medical needs. As we close this chapter on the struggles and barriers faced by patients in accessing care, we reflect on the imperative to address these issues holistically. It's not sufficient to acknowledge these barriers; active, systemic changes are required to dismantle them. Moving forward into the next chapter, the focus shifts to understanding and addressing drug safety and efficacy concerns, a topic that intertwines closely with the issues of access and equity, continuing our exploration of the critical challenges within the healthcare system.

6

Chapter 5 Drug Safety and Efficacy Concerns

Imagine, for a moment, that you or a loved one has been prescribed a new medication. There is a sense of relief and hope that this treatment may address persistent health challenges. However, weeks later, news breaks that the medication has been recalled due to severe, unforeseen side effects. Such scenarios are not just disturbing; they underscore the critical importance of drug safety and the sometimes catastrophic consequences when it is compromised. This chapter delves into the multifaceted world of drug safety and efficacy, unraveling the complexities behind drug recalls, adverse reactions, the role of surveillance post-market, and the vital part played by patient advocacy groups in safeguarding public health.

5.1 When Medications Harm

Case Studies of Drug Recalls

Though relatively rare, drug recalls can be high-profile events that shake public trust in pharmaceutical safety protocols. One poignant example involves a popular arthritis medication that was withdrawn globally after studies linked it to an increased risk of heart attacks and strokes. The recall was not immediate; it came only after millions had been prescribed the medication, believing it safe. Analysis of what went wrong indicates a lapse in the initial clinical trials, where cardiovascular risks were inadequately assessed. Furthermore, post-market surveillance was insufficient, as the drug was widely marketed and consumed before long-term risks were fully understood. The impact on patients was profound, not just physically but emotionally, as they grappled with the betrayal of trust and the realization that their health had been compromised by systemic failures in drug safety oversight.

Adverse Drug Reactions

Adverse drug reactions (ADRs) are more common than many realize and can range from mild allergic reactions to severe and life-threatening responses. The prevalence of such reactions poses a significant public health challenge. For instance, antibiotics are widely used and generally considered safe. However, they are also a leading cause of severe ADRs that can lead to hospitalizations or require significant medical interventions. The impact of ADRs extends beyond the immediate health effects; they have a ripple effect on healthcare resources, patient quality of life, and overall healthcare costs. Understanding these reactions, their root causes, and potential risk factors is critical for minimizing harm and protecting patient health.

Lack of Post-Market Surveillance

The oversight of a drug continues once it hits the market; post-market surveillance is crucial to ensure continued safety and efficacy. However, the systems in place for monitoring drugs after approval often need to be more funded and staffed, leading to gaps in safety oversight. For example, a particular diabetes medication was found to cause severe and sometimes fatal skin reactions. This side effect was rare and not detected in clinical trials but only came to light after the drug had been in use for several years. This delay in recognition and response highlights the critical gaps in our current post-market surveillance systems, underscoring the need for more robust mechanisms to monitor drugs throughout their lifecycle on the market.

Patient Advocacy for Safety

In the face of these challenges, patient advocacy groups play an indispensable role. These groups support and educate patients and lobby for stricter safety regulations and more transparent processes from pharmaceutical companies and regulatory bodies. Their advocacy efforts have led to significant changes in drug safety policies, including implementing more stringent post-market surveillance practices and requiring more transparent labeling of potential side effects. The work of these groups highlights the power of informed and organized patient communities in driving change, ensuring that drug safety remains a top priority in healthcare policy and practice.

Exploring the terrain of drug safety through the lens of recalls, adverse reactions, surveillance shortcomings, and advocacy illuminates the pivotal challenges and actions needed to protect public health. As we navigate these complex issues, it becomes clear that ensuring drug safety is not just a regulatory obligation but a shared responsibility that calls for vigilance, transparency, and proactive engagement from all stakeholders involved.

5.2 The Efficacy Illusion

In the realm of modern medicine, the efficacy of a drug is often presented as a straightforward fact supported by rigorous clinical trials and robust data. However, the reality can sometimes be less clear-cut. The benefits of certain medications are frequently overstated, a phenomenon rooted in selective reporting of trial results and, sometimes, misleading marketing practices. This manipulation of data can significantly alter the perceived effectiveness of a medication, leading patients and healthcare providers to make treatment decisions based on skewed information. For instance, in some scenarios, pharmaceutical companies may release only those study results that show a positive outcome while underreporting or altogether omitting trials where the drug performed poorly or was found to be no more effective than a placebo. This selective data dissemination distorts the drug's true efficacy and considerably complicates the treatment landscape.

The issue of overstated benefits is particularly pertinent in the management of chronic diseases, where long-term medication is often a key component of treatment. The efficacy of medications in these contexts is crucial because they are not just about alleviating symptoms momentarily; they are about managing a condition over a lifetime. Take, for example, the widespread use of certain blockbuster drugs for diabetes and heart disease. While these medications are effective in managing symptoms and are indeed life-saving for many, there is an ongoing debate about whether they adequately address the underlying causes of these diseases or merely mask symptoms. This distinction is critical because it shapes not just individual treatment plans but broader public health policies and healthcare spending. When medications predominantly manage symptoms without altering the disease course, patients may become dependent on these drugs for life, which can be immensely profitable for drug manufacturers but raises questions about the sustainability and holistic management of health.

The debate surrounding the efficacy of psychiatric medications brings additional layers of complexity to this discussion. Psychiatric drugs, including antidepressants and antipsychotics, are among the most prescribed medications worldwide. However, their long-term efficacy and dependency issues are subjects of intense debate. Critics argue that while these medications can be effective in providing short-term relief from mental health symptoms, their long-term use may lead to dependency and could potentially exacerbate symptoms or lead to additional health problems. Moreover, the biological underpinnings of psychiatric conditions are often not as well understood as those of physical ailments, making the efficacy of psychiatric drugs a particularly contentious issue. This ongoing debate underscores the necessity for a nuanced approach to psychiatric treatment, one that considers both the potential benefits and the risks of long-term medication use.

Amidst these complexities, the importance of informed decision-making becomes ever more apparent. As a patient or a caregiver, you must navigate this intricate landscape with access to transparent and unbiased information about the medications being considered. This means having access to the glossy brochures, persuasive sales pitches, and the raw data from clinical trials, including those that still need to make it to the press releases. It also means understanding the statistical significance and the clinical relevance of the results presented and discerning the difference between a statistically significant outcome and one meaningful in real-life terms. For instance, a medication that claims to reduce the risk of a heart attack by 30% might sound impressive. However, if the actual risk of having a heart attack is very low, the absolute benefit might be minimal, a nuance that might get lost in the bold headlines.

Navigating these issues requires a proactive stance, seeking out resources that offer balanced and comprehensive analyses of medication efficacy. It involves consulting with healthcare providers who are willing to discuss not just the benefits but also the limitations of prescribed treatments. Above all, it demands a critical eye and a willingness to question and learn, traits that are indispensable in a landscape where the efficacy of medications can sometimes be an illusion, shaped as much by commercial interests as by scientific evidence. As you continue to engage with your healthcare journey, remember that understanding the true efficacy of medications is not just about reading data but about reading between the lines, where the real story often lies.

5.3 Alternatives on the Fringe: The Debate Over Non-Traditional Treatments

The landscape of healthcare is witnessing a burgeoning interest in alternative treatments, which encompass a broad spectrum of therapies outside conventional Western medicine. These treatments range from herbal supplements and acupuncture to recent innovations like biofeedback and aromatherapy. The allure of these alternatives often lies in their perceived gentleness, promise of fewer side effects, and a more holistic approach to treating the individual rather than just the symptoms. However, as these therapies gain popularity, it becomes imperative to scrutinize their efficacy and safety through the lens of evidence-based practice.

The rise of alternative treatments can be seen as a response to growing dissatisfaction with conventional medicine's ability to manage chronic conditions and its often impersonal approach. Many patients are turning to options like acupuncture, which has roots extending thousands of years back in Chinese medicine, to manage pain and stress. Herbal supplements, too, are gaining traction, driven by a desire to treat ailments with natural products rather than synthetic medications. While the motivations for exploring these alternatives are well-founded, the critical issue remains the variable quality and sometimes dubious efficacy of these treatments. With rigorous scientific evaluation, it's easier to differentiate between what genuinely benefits patients and what might even cause harm due to a lack of standardized preparation and dosing.

The importance of evidence-based practice in evaluating these treatments must be considered. Evidence-based practice involves integrating individual clinical expertise with the best available external clinical evidence from systematic research. For alternative therapies, this means rigorous randomized controlled trials, meta-analyses, and systematic reviews to ascertain both efficacy and safety. For instance, while certain herbal supplements are touted for their ability to improve everything from memory to stamina, they may also interact adversely with prescription medications or lead to toxic side effects if not used correctly. Healthcare providers and researchers are responsible for conducting and disseminating research that can guide safe and effective use.

Integrative medicine approaches symbolize a bridge between conventional and alternative treatments, offering a comprehensive model that combines the best of both worlds. This approach enhances the therapeutic relationship between patient and provider and personalizes treatment plans to fit the unique set of circumstances each patient presents. For example, a patient undergoing cancer treatment might receive chemotherapy alongside acupuncture to help manage side effects like nausea and pain, thereby improving quality of life and possibly enhancing the efficacy of conventional treatment protocols. The potential benefits of integrative approaches are vast. Still, they require a collaborative effort among healthcare professionals trained in a variety of disciplines to ensure that all treatments provided are safe and coordinated effectively.

Navigating misinformation and marketing claims about alternative treatments is another challenge that you might face as a patient. The market is saturated with products and therapies claiming miraculous cures and rapid health benefits. To critically evaluate these claims, it is vital to seek information from reliable sources—such as peer-reviewed journals, reputable medical organizations, and trained healthcare professionals. Consulting with a healthcare provider not only helps in assessing the credibility of a treatment but also ensures that it does not interfere with other ongoing treatments. Awareness and education are your best defenses against the pitfalls of misinformation, empowering you to make informed choices about your health.

As the chapter on drug safety and efficacy concerns comes to a close, we reflect on the complex interplay between conventional medications and alternative treatments in today's healthcare landscape. From understanding the rigorous scrutiny necessary to validate the safety of pharmaceuticals to recognizing the potential of integrative approaches, the journey through this chapter underscores the necessity for a balanced, well-informed perspective on all available treatment options. Moving forward, the exploration continues into the realm of patient rights and advocacies, where the focus shifts to empowering you with knowledge and tools to navigate the healthcare system effectively.

Chapter 6 The Quest for Solutions

Navigating the healthcare system often feels akin to solving a complex puzzle where the pieces don't fit together effortlessly. Among these pieces, insurance coverage is one of the most convoluted elements, riddled with fine print and often labyrinthine stipulations that can confound even the most astute individuals. This chapter is devoted to arming you with the necessary tools and insights to understand and effectively navigate this challenging aspect of healthcare, ensuring that you can advocate for your health needs without succumbing to common pitfalls.

6.1 Navigating Insurance Nightmares

Understanding Your Policy

The first step in conquering insurance challenges is to understand your policy thoroughly. This is not merely about knowing what your monthly premium costs but grasping the nitty-gritty details that dictate what and how much the insurance covers. Key terms such as "deductible," "out-of-pocket maximum," "co-payment," and "coinsurance" are not just jargon; they are crucial metrics that determine your financial responsibility in medical scenarios. For instance, a "deductible" is the amount you pay for covered health care services before your insurance plan starts to pay. Knowing the specifics of these terms can prevent unexpected expenses and prepare you for potential financial planning.

Moreover, it's essential to understand the nuances of your policy's coverage details, such as the differences between in-network and out-of-network services. In-network providers have contracted with your health plan to provide services at a negotiated rate, which typically means lower costs for you. On the other hand, receiving care from out-of-network providers can lead to significantly higher charges, as these do not have pre-negotiated rates with your insurer. By comprehending these distinctions, you can make informed decisions about where to receive care, potentially saving thousands of dollars in medical bills.

Disputing Insurance Decisions

At times, you might find yourself in a position where your insurance provider denies coverage for a treatment your healthcare provider deems necessary. In such instances, knowing how to dispute insurance decisions is imperative. Begin by thoroughly reviewing the denial letter, which should explain why the claim was denied and how you can appeal the decision. It's crucial to act swiftly, as appeals have a limited window to file them.

When preparing your appeal, gather all relevant medical records, doctors' notes, and any supporting literature that underscores the necessity of the treatment. A detailed letter from your healthcare provider explaining why the treatment is essential can be particularly persuasive. Maintaining organized records and persistent follow-up can increase your chances of overturning the denial throughout this process. Remember, insurance companies are required by law to have an appeals process, and understanding this process can empower you to advocate effectively for your healthcare needs.

Alternative Insurance Options

Exploring alternative insurance options can provide solutions tailored more closely to individual needs or financial situations. Health-sharing ministries and high-deductible health plans are examples of such alternatives. Health-sharing ministries are not insurance providers but cooperatives that pool money to share medical expenses among members who share ethical or religious beliefs. While often more affordable, they may not guarantee coverage and typically do not cover pre-existing conditions, making them a less viable option for some.

Conversely, high-deductible health plans (HDHPs) offer lower monthly premiums but require you to pay more out-of-pocket before the insurance kicks in. These plans can be beneficial if you are generally healthy and primarily need coverage for catastrophic events. However, they can be financially burdensome if you require frequent medical care. Weighing the pros and cons of these alternatives against your health needs and financial ability is crucial in making an informed decision that aligns with your circumstances.

Preventive Care and Wellness

Emphasizing preventive care and wellness programs is essential for maintaining health and reducing long-term healthcare costs. Preventive services — screenings, immunizations, and regular check-ups — can detect health issues early when they are typically easier and less expensive to treat. Engaging in wellness programs, which often include activities like health education classes, fitness memberships, and nutrition counseling, can further bolster your health, potentially averting costly medical interventions in the future.

Many insurance plans, especially following the Affordable Care Act, provide coverage for preventive services without copayments or coinsurance, even if you still need to meet your deductible. Taking full advantage of these benefits supports your long-term health and aligns with financially savvy healthcare management. Engaging actively in your health optimizes your well-being. It constructs a foundation that could minimize your need for more intensive medical interventions, a win-win scenario in both health and financial terms.

As we continue to unravel the complexities of navigating insurance and exploring all avenues to safeguard health and manage costs effectively, it becomes increasingly clear that being well-informed and proactive are your best strategies. This chapter serves as a guide but also as a reminder of the power you hold in

53

managing your healthcare journey through informed decisions and active participation.

6.2 Advocacy and Rights: Empowering the Patient

In the intricate web of healthcare, knowing your rights is not just beneficial; it's critical to navigating the system effectively and ensuring that your health needs are met with respect and diligence. The Patient Bill of Rights, a pivotal element in healthcare, serves as a guardian of your rights, ensuring that your healthcare experience is effective but also humane and respectful. This set of rights outlines what you, as a patient, are entitled to in the healthcare environment, including the right to receive accurate information, to make autonomous decisions about your treatment options, and to be treated with respect and without discrimination.

Understanding these rights is fundamental. For instance, you have the right to be informed about the risks and benefits of all treatment options, which empowers you to make decisions based on comprehensive information. This right supports your autonomy and ensures you participate actively in your healthcare decisions rather than being passive recipients. Moreover, the right to privacy concerning your medical records is crucial in maintaining your dignity and trust in the healthcare process, ensuring that sensitive information is shared only with your consent and for your benefit.

Equally important is knowing how to advocate for yourself

within this framework. Effective self-advocacy starts with clear communication with your healthcare providers. Preparing for appointments with specific questions or concerns about your condition or treatment options is essential. This preparation makes the conversation more productive and ensures that you can express your needs and preferences clearly. Always remember that you are entitled to ask for explanations or further details until you fully understand the information provided. This might include asking for clarification on medical jargon or the implications of potential side effects of a proposed treatment.

Navigating the healthcare bureaucracy is another crucial skill that can significantly enhance your ability to manage your healthcare effectively. This includes understanding how to schedule appointments efficiently, how to obtain and under-stand your medical records, and how to follow up on test results or referrals. Managing these tasks proactively can prevent delays in receiving care and ensure you are fully informed about your health status. For example, knowing how to access your medical records electronically can help you track your health history and share important health information with various providers, thereby improving the coordination of your care.

Legal resources and support services provide a safety net for when things go awry, such as medical malpractice cases or insurance coverage disputes. Knowing where to find legal advice or how to access patient advocacy services can be invaluable. Organizations such as the Patient Advocate Foundation or local legal aid societies can offer guidance and support, helping you to navigate legal challenges effectively. These resources ensure that you are not alone in addressing complex legal issues that may arise, providing support and advocacy to uphold your rights and interests.

In empowering yourself with the knowledge of your rights and the strategies for advocacy, you are better prepared to face the healthcare system not as a bystander but as a key participant. This empowerment not only enhances your ability to secure the best possible care for yourself but also contributes to a more patient-centered healthcare system where the rights and needs of patients are at the forefront of healthcare delivery. As you continue to engage with the system, remember that your voice is powerful, your rights are safeguarded, and your ability to advocate for yourself is a significant determinant of your healthcare experience.

6.3 The Digital Health Revolution

The landscape of healthcare is undergoing a profound transformation, driven by the integration of digital technologies that promise to enhance the efficiency and personalization of care. Among these innovations, telehealth services have surged to the forefront, particularly highlighted by their indispensable role during the COVID-19 pandemic. Telehealth, or telemedicine, utilizes digital communication tools to deliver clinical services to patients without an in-person visit. This technology has revolutionized access to care, particularly for individuals in remote or underserved areas, where traditional healthcare services might be scarce or difficult to access. The convenience of consulting with a healthcare provider from the comfort of one's home is appealing. It reduces travel time and associated costs, making it easier for patients to manage regular appointments and maintain continuous care regimes.

Moreover, telehealth has proven to be a critical resource for managing chronic conditions, where frequent monitoring and regular consultations are necessary. Patients with diabetes, for example, can benefit from regular virtual check-ins with their healthcare providers to discuss blood sugar levels and insulin management without the need for frequent, time-consuming trips to the doctor's office. Additionally, telehealth services have expanded to include mental health therapies, offering sessions via video calls, which has been particularly crucial in addressing the increased mental health challenges posed by the isolation and stress of the pandemic. The flexibility and accessibility of telehealth not only enhance patient engagement and satisfaction but also contribute to better patient outcomes, as the ease of access can lead to more consistent care and adherence to treatment plans.

The role of health apps and monitoring devices in managing health is another pivotal component of the digital health revolution. These tools range from basic fitness trackers monitoring steps and physical activity to more advanced systems tracking heart rate, sleep patterns, and even blood glucose levels. Integrating health apps into daily life allows individuals to take a more active role in managing their wellness and preventive care. For instance, apps that provide medication reminders or that track medication adherence can be particularly beneficial for patients managing multiple medications, ensuring they take the proper dosage at the correct times, thus preventing potential health complications.

Furthermore, these apps often allow users to collect and analyze data regarding their health behaviors, offering insights that can lead to healthier lifestyle choices. For example, a simple app tracking water intake can motivate an individual to achieve daily hydration goals, a small but significant step towards better health. The data collected can also be shared with healthcare providers during consultations, providing a more comprehensive view of the patient's daily habits and health status, which can inform more personalized and effective treatment plans.

Electronic Health Records (EHRs) represent a foundational element of modern healthcare informatics, significantly impacting patient care by improving the coordination and efficiency of healthcare services. EHRs allow for the seamless exchange of patient information among different healthcare providers, ensuring that regardless of the location, the provider can access a patient's complete medical history. This accessibility is crucial for emergency care, where time-sensitive decisions need to be made quickly and with a complete understanding of the patient's medical background. Additionally, EHRs facilitate a more holistic view of patient health, promoting preventive care and more coordinated management of chronic diseases. Patients can benefit from this integrated approach, which tends to be more comprehensive and proactive in maintaining patient health over time.

Digital health literacy is a critical enabler in this technological shift, ensuring that patients can access digital health tools and use them effectively. Understanding how to navigate health apps, interpret the data provided by health monitoring devices, and interact with telehealth platforms is essential for patients to benefit fully from these technologies. Moreover, as health data becomes increasingly digital, patients need to be aware of how to manage and protect their personal health information. Educating patients on digital health literacy helps bridge the gap between technology availability and effective use, empowering them to participate actively in their health management and decision-making processes.

As we wrap up our exploration of the digital health revolution, we reflect on how these technologies are not just changing medical practices but are also deeply influencing patient experiences and expectations. The shift towards more patient-centered, technology-enabled care promises more personalized, accessible, and effective healthcare. By embracing these innovations, patients are not just passive recipients of care but active participants in managing their health, equipped with tools that foster greater autonomy and engagement. As we transition from this chapter, we carry forward the understanding that when effectively integrated into healthcare, technology can significantly enhance the quality and accessibility of care, paving the way for a healthier, more empowered society.

8

Chapter 7 The Quest for Solutions

In the vast and intricate world of healthcare, envisioning reform is akin to steering a colossal ship through uncharted waters— the task is daunting yet essential for reaching safer, more equitable harbors. As we delve into this exploration, it is vital to recognize that no single model of healthcare reform is universally applicable; instead, effective strategies can often be found in the diversity of systems practiced around the globe. In this chapter, we look outward to understand how different nations have sculpted their healthcare landscapes, extracting valuable lessons that could illuminate paths to reform in the United States.

7.1 Models of Success: Learning from Around the World

The quest for a more efficient and equitable healthcare system has led numerous countries to adopt varied models, each with nuances and successes. By examining systems like those in

Canada, Germany, and Japan, we can distill principles and practices that enhance the quality of care and ensure it is delivered cost-effectively and fairly.

Comparative Analysis

Canada, Germany, and Japan exemplify different facets of healthcare excellence. Canada's healthcare system, known for its public funding and private delivery, offers a compelling model of universal health coverage that ensures all citizens have access to necessary healthcare services without financial hardship. The system's cornerstone is its commitment to accessibility and universality, principles deeply embedded in the Canadian Health Act. Meanwhile, Germany's health insurance system operates under a "sickness fund" model where both employers and employees contribute. This system is distinguished by its negotiation between sickness funds and healthcare providers to set prices, a practice that maintains competitive costs while ensuring high standards of care. In contrast, Japan offers a unique mix of employer-based and community-based insurance, ensuring that everyone—from children to the elderly—receives care. The Japanese system is particularly noteworthy for its emphasis on preventive care and health education, contributing to the country's high life expectancy.

Cost Efficiency and Quality of Care

Efficiency in healthcare is not merely about reducing costs but doing so in a way that maintains, if not enhances, the quality of care. Germany's model exemplifies this balance. By standardizing prices across the board and allowing free choice of providers, the system avoids the pitfall of low-quality care that might arise from cost-cutting measures. Similarly, Japan's focus on preventive care—a strategy that reduces the need for expensive treatments for preventable diseases—exemplifies how upstream investments in health can result in downstream savings. These models underscore the principle that cost efficiency should not compromise the quality of care but should enhance it through strategic planning and preventive practices.

Universal Coverage Success Stories

The success stories of universal coverage from these countries are not just about health statistics but about the impact on individuals' lives. In Canada, universal coverage means no individual has to face bankruptcy due to medical bills, a significant source of stress and financial instability in countries without such coverage. In Germany, the extensive network of providers ensures that no citizen is left without care, promoting a healthier, more productive society. Japan's comprehensive coverage, even in remote areas, ensures that all citizens have access to the healthcare services they need, contributing to the nation's low infant mortality rate and long life expectancy. These stories highlight the profound societal benefits that can arise from a well-structured universal healthcare system.

Adaptation Lessons

Adapting these international lessons to the U.S. requires careful consideration of cultural, economic, and political factors. However, the core principles of these successful models—universal coverage, cost efficiency, and a focus on preventive care—offer a blueprint for reform. Implementing these principles in the U.S. could involve expanding Medicare to cover all citizens, thereby ensuring universal coverage. Introducing more rigorous price negotiations between healthcare providers and insurers, similar to the German model, could help control costs. Moreover, increasing investments in preventive care and health education, inspired by Japan, could reduce the long-term demands on the healthcare system.

As we continue to explore the possibilities of healthcare reform, understanding these international models offers a glimpse into what is achievable and a roadmap of practices that could be tailored to meet the unique needs of the U.S. healthcare landscape. By learning from global successes and challenges, we can better navigate the complexities of healthcare reform, aiming for a system that upholds the ideals of equity, quality, and efficiency.

7.2 The Single-Payer Proposal: Pros and Cons

A single-payer system, often discussed in the context of health-care reform, represents a design where one entity—usually a governmental body—handles the collection of all healthcare fees and the disbursement of all healthcare costs. Within such a framework, the government essentially becomes the sole "payer" covering medical expenses for all residents, funded through taxes, eliminating the need for private health insurance. In the United States, implementing a single-payer system would mean a significant overhaul of the current multi-payer system, which includes private insurance companies, state healthcare providers, and federal programs like Medicare and Medicaid.

The potential benefits of transitioning to a single-payer system are substantial. Firstly, administrative simplicity stands out. By consolidating the administration of healthcare funds and claims under one umbrella, the system can reduce the overhead costs associated with managing multiple insurers and plans. This streamlined approach cuts down on bureaucratic layers. It reduces confusion for providers and patients, who must navigate a complex web of insurers, each with its rules and coverage limits. Moreover, a single-payer system inherently promises universal coverage, ensuring that all individuals access necessary healthcare services regardless of their economic status or background. This universality can be a significant stride towards achieving health equity, addressing gaps currently leaving millions uninsured or underinsured.

Furthermore, the economic scale of a single-payer system could drive down overall healthcare costs. With the government as the sole payer, it would have a greater ability to negotiate and regulate prices with healthcare providers and pharmaceutical companies, potentially leading to lower costs for services and medications. These savings could then be redirected towards enhancing the quality of care or expanding services to more effectively meet the needs of the population.

However, the transition to a single-payer system is fraught with challenges and criticisms. One of the most significant concerns is the financial burden such a system might impose on taxpayers.

Adequately Funding a single-payer system requires substantial tax increases, which could be unpopular and politically challenging. The prospect of higher taxes raises concerns about the economic impact on individuals and businesses. It sparks debate about the government's role in providing services traditionally handled by the private sector.

Moreover, critics argue that a single-payer system could decrease healthcare innovation incentives. With the government controlling payments and setting prices, there could be less motivation for providers and pharmaceutical companies to innovate and improve services. Furthermore, such a system might lead to increased demand for healthcare services, potentially resulting in longer wait times and decreased quality of care if not managed effectively. The balance between providing universal health coverage and maintaining high standards of care is delicate and complex, requiring careful planning and robust systems to manage the increased load on healthcare resources.

The differences become stark when comparing the single-payer proposal with other systems, particularly those with mixed models involving both government and private insurers. Systems with multiple payers can offer a variety of plans with different levels of coverage, potentially catering to individual preferences and needs more effectively than a one-size-fits-all government plan. However, due to their complexity, these systems often need help with higher administrative costs and inefficiencies. In contrast, a single-payer system simplifies the landscape at the expense of reduced flexibility and choice for consumers. Each system has its unique advantages and drawbacks, and the choice between them often reflects broader societal values and priorities regarding freedom of choice, equity in access to services, and the role of government in citizens' lives.

As we consider the future of healthcare in the United States, the debate over the single-payer system underscores the broader challenges of reforming a sector as complex and vital as health-care. The discussion extends beyond economic calculations and political feasibility; it touches on fundamental questions about how we value health and healthcare access as integral components of societal well-being.

7.3 Cutting the Middlemen: Direct Primary Care and Beyond

In the evolving narrative of healthcare reform, Direct Primary Care (DPC) emerges as a compelling chapter that redefines the patient-doctor relationship by stripping away some of the most cumbersome layers of traditional insurance-based models. DPC is a straightforward arrangement where you pay a flat monthly fee directly to your primary care provider. This fee covers most, if not all, primary care services, including clinical, laboratory, and consultative services, and sometimes even medications and minor procedures. The model operates on a membership basis, akin to a subscription, emphasizing preventive care and enhanced access to doctors.

One of the most significant benefits of Direct Primary Care is the personalized attention it affords. With DPC, doctors typically manage fewer patients than their counterparts in traditional settings. This smaller patient load translates into more time spent with each patient during visits, allowing for comprehensive discussions about health concerns without the usual rush to move on to the next appointment. This model enhances the quality of care and strengthens the patient-doctor relationship, fostering a level of trust and familiarity that can be crucial in managing long-term health outcomes.

Furthermore, the transparency in pricing associated with DPC eliminates much of the unpredictability surrounding healthcare costs. Traditional insurance often involves co-pays, deductibles, and other out-of-pocket expenses that vary widely depending on the treatment. DPC simplifies this to a single monthly fee that covers most primary care services, making healthcare expenses predictable and often more affordable over the long term. Additionally, this model can significantly reduce the time and resources spent navigating insurance bureaucracy, allowing healthcare providers to focus more on patient care rather than paperwork.

Beyond Direct Primary Care, other innovative delivery models are making inroads to streamline healthcare provision. Medical cooperatives, for instance, bring together groups of patients who, much like in DPC, pay a flat monthly fee for access to a wide array of healthcare services. These cooperatives often extend beyond primary care, including specialized services negotiated at discounted rates with network providers. This model broadens access to comprehensive healthcare and fosters a community-oriented approach to health management, where patients and providers share a mutual interest in optimizing health outcomes.

Integrated health systems represent another progressive model, where multiple healthcare aspects— from primary care to specialty services and hospital care—are coordinated under a single organizational umbrella. This integration eliminates the redundancies and inefficiencies often associated with fragmented healthcare provision. By ensuring that all caregivers are on the same page and that health records are seamlessly shared across disciplines, these systems enhance the quality of care and patient safety while potentially reducing costs through improved efficiency.

Despite these models' promising benefits, they need help scaling and integrating within the broader healthcare system. The primary hurdle is the ingrained structure of the existing healthcare landscape, which relies heavily on traditional insurance and fee-for-service models. Transitioning to DPC or other innovative models requires changes at the practice level, shifts in patient perception, and regulatory adjustments. Moreover, these models must demonstrate that they can provide comprehensive care, including for severe and chronic conditions, to broader sections of the population.

Opportunities for future growth in these models are substantial. As more data demonstrates the benefits of these care models in terms of patient satisfaction, health outcomes, and cost savings, resistance to change may diminish. Policy innovations, such as allowing DPC to be paid for with pre-tax dollars or integrating these models more fully with Medicare and Medicaid, could accelerate their adoption. The ongoing digitization of healthcare, with advancements in telehealth and health informatics, also offers synergistic tools that can enhance the effectiveness and reach of these models.

Direct Primary Care and other innovative healthcare delivery models represent a shift in how care is provided and a
reimagining of the patient-provider relationship. They offer
a path toward a more personalized, transparent, and efficient
healthcare system, aligning closely with the needs and preferences of patients while potentially reducing overall healthcare
expenditures. As we conclude this exploration of cutting-edge
healthcare models, it's clear that the journey towards a reformed
healthcare system is multifaceted and ongoing, requiring continuous adaptation and commitment to the principles of quality,
accessibility, and patient-centered care.

Chapter 8 The Role of Innovation and Technology

In healthcare, the winds of change are increasingly powered by the sails of innovation and technology. As we venture further into this chapter, you will discover how biotechnological breakthroughs are not just reshaping what we thought was possible in medicine but also challenging us to rethink the ethical frameworks and accessibility of cutting-edge treatments. The promise of these technologies brings a shimmer of hope, yet it is shadowed by significant challenges that must be navigated with both caution and optimism.

8.1 Breakthroughs in Biotechnology: Promises and Pitfalls

Gene Editing and CRISPR

Imagine a world where genetic diseases, once thought to be life sentences, could be edited out of your DNA, much like correcting typos in a document. This is no longer the stuff of science fiction, thanks to revolutionary advancements in gene editing technologies such as CRISPR (Clustered Regularly Interspaced Short Palindromic Repeats). CRISPR has transformed genetic research landscape by allowing scientists to edit parts of the genome with unprecedented precision, efficiency, and flexibility. At its core, CRISPR is a tool that can be programmed to target specific stretches of genetic code and to edit DNA at precise locations. Researchers are harnessing this capability to correct genetic defects, treat and prevent the spread of diseases, and improve crops. However, the ability to alter DNA raises substantial ethical questions. The idea of "designer babies," where embryos could potentially be edited to enhance aesthetic features, intelligence, or physical ability, poses significant moral and societal dilemmas. The technology is promising for treating genetic disorders, yet it opens Pandora's box of ethical considerations that society must manage carefully.

Regenerative Medicine

Moving from the microscopic to the macroscopic, regenerative medicine is a branch of medicine that aims to repair or replace tissue and organs damaged by age, disease, or trauma. This field harnesses the body's regenerative capabilities and uses a combination of tissue engineering, cellular therapies, medical devices, and artificial organs. Among the most groundbreaking developments in this area is stem cell therapy, which involves using stem cells to regenerate damaged tissues and organs. Another area is organ regeneration, which could end the transplant shortage by growing organs in the lab. The implications for patient care are profound, offering possibilities for recovery

71

that were once deemed unattainable. However, the road to regular clinical use of these therapies is fraught with technical challenges and ethical issues concerning stem cell sourcing and the potential for organ rejection.

Ethical Considerations

As we delve deeper into the capabilities of biotechnology, it becomes imperative to discuss the ethical landscapes these technologies navigate. The rapid advancements in biotech challenge our current understanding of medicine and push the boundaries of what is ethically acceptable in treatment and enhancement. Ethical considerations range from concerns about equity in access to these technologies to debates over what constitutes normal versus enhanced human capabilities. As these technologies can potentially create divides in society, it is crucial to consider how they can be developed and implemented in ways that do not exacerbate social inequalities.

Accessibility and Equity

A pivotal challenge facing the deployment of biotechnological innovations is ensuring they benefit all of humanity, not just a privileged few. Accessibility and equity in healthcare technology are critical issues that need addressing to prevent a scenario where advanced treatments become luxuries only the wealthy can afford. For instance, while gene editing offers potential cures for genetic diseases, the cost of such treatments could be prohibitively high, limiting access based on socioeconomic status. Similarly, regenerative medicine treatments, such as custom-grown organs or specialized stem cell therapies, might carry hefty price tags that could make them inaccessible to underprivileged populations. This disparity raises significant concerns about the widening gap between different segments of society regarding access to advanced medical care.

As we navigate the promises and pitfalls of biotechnological innovations, it remains clear that while the potential to cure diseases and even fundamentally enhance human abilities is tantalizing, the journey there is lined with complex ethical debates and significant challenges in ensuring equitable access. These innovations beckon a future of immense possibilities and responsibilities, reminding us that with great power comes great responsibility. The decisions we make today concerning the development and use of these technologies will shape not just the future of medicine but the very fabric of society itself.

8.2 Artificial Intelligence in Diagnosis and Treatment

Artificial Intelligence (AI) and machine learning are not just buzzwords but are increasingly becoming integral components of modern healthcare, revolutionizing how diagnoses are made and treatments are administered. By harnessing vast amounts of healthcare data and learning from it, these technologies significantly enhance diagnostic accuracy and the speed at which it is achieved. In medical imaging, for instance, AI algorithms are employed to analyze X-rays, MRIs, and CT scans with precision and efficiency that surpasses even the most trained human eyes. The advantage of AI in this field lies in its ability to detect subtle patterns and anomalies that might be overlooked in manual evaluations. For example, AI systems have been developed to identify signs of diseases such as pneumonia or breast cancer from imaging scans with remarkable accuracy, often detecting early-stage signs critical for successful treatment outcomes. Moreover, AI transforms tissue analysis in pathology, helping pathologists identify and characterize diseases from tissue samples more quickly and accurately. This leap in diagnostic capabilities could mean earlier interventions, personalized treatment approaches, and better patient outcomes.

The role of AI extends beyond diagnostics into the personalization of treatment plans. Tailored treatment is the cornerstone of adequate healthcare, and AI is pivotal in making personalized medicine more of a reality than ever before. By analyzing a patient's unique health data—ranging from genetic information to lifestyle factors—AI algorithms can help predict how they will respond to various treatments. This capability allows healthcare providers to devise highly customized treatment plans, maximizing efficacy while minimizing side effects. For patients with complex conditions like cancer, where the interplay of genetic factors and disease characteristics can vary widely between individuals, AI-driven personalized treatment plans represent a significant advancement. These AI systems can analyze data from past treatment outcomes, current research, and individual patient responses to suggest the most effective therapies, thereby improving the quality of life for patients and enhancing survival rates.

Furthermore, AI is making significant inroads in streamlining administrative processes within healthcare settings, which, while less visible to patients, is crucial for enhancing the overall efficiency and patient experience in healthcare facilities. Administrative tasks in healthcare are notoriously time-consuming and prone to human error, encompassing everything from scheduling appointments to processing insurance claims and managing patient records. AI is adept at automating these processes, significantly reducing the time healthcare staff need on routine tasks and allowing them more time to focus on patient care. For example, AI-driven systems can predict peak times for patient visits and help schedule staff accordingly, optimizing both human and physical resources in hospitals and clinics. Moreover, by automating insurance claims processing, AI can reduce errors and speed up reimbursements. This benefit indirectly contributes to patient satisfaction by ensuring smoother, more efficient interactions with healthcare providers.

However, as with all powerful tools, the use of AI in healthcare comes with its set of ethical and privacy concerns that must be diligently addressed. The foremost problem is data security. Healthcare data is extremely sensitive, and the proliferation of AI applications increases the risk of breaches. Protecting this data from unauthorized access is paramount, requiring robust, constantly updated cybersecurity measures to keep pace with evolving threats. Furthermore, the issue of algorithmic bias presents another significant challenge. AI systems are only as unbiased as the data on which they are trained. If this data reflects existing prejudices, these biases can be perpetuated and amplified, leading to disparities in healthcare delivery. For instance, if an AI system is trained predominantly with data from one demographic, its accuracy might decrease when applied to a different demographic, potentially leading to misdiagnoses or suboptimal care. Addressing these biases requires a concerted effort to ensure that AI training datasets are diverse and representative of all populations to whom the AI will be applied.

In navigating these promising yet challenging waters of AI in healthcare, it becomes clear that while AI can transform many aspects of patient diagnosis and treatment, it also necessitates a careful balance between innovation and ethical responsibility. Ensuring that AI is used judiciously and ethically, with a steadfast focus on enhancing patient care and protecting patient data, will be crucial as we integrate these advanced technologies into everyday healthcare practices.

8.3 The Blockchain Revolution in Healthcare Data

In an era where data breaches regularly make headlines, the imperative for robust data security measures in healthcare is more pressing than ever. Blockchain technology, initially devised for digital currency transactions, offers a novel approach to securing and managing healthcare data. At its core, blockchain is a distributed database that allows data to be stored globally on thousands of servers while letting anyone on the network see everyone else's entries in real-time. This makes it exceptionally secure and incredibly difficult for any single party to take control of the entire blockchain or alter its records retroactively.

In healthcare, the application of blockchain technology can revolutionize how patient data is handled, enhancing both security and privacy. Traditional databases centralize data storage, creating a single point of failure that hackers can target. Blockchain disperses this data across an entire network, significantly mitigating the risk of data breaches. Each 'block' of data is linked to the previous one and secured using cryptographic principles, ensuring each entry is tamper-evident and immutable. This level of security is paramount in healthcare, where protecting sensitive patient information is not just a regulatory requirement but a fundamental aspect of patient trust and safety.

Furthermore, blockchain technology can substantially enhance the privacy of patient data. Through decentralized networks, blockchain allows for creating comprehensive and immutable audit trails. This means every access to the data is recorded, and unauthorized attempts to access data can be detected in real time. Patients can be provided with keys to control who can view their data, enhancing patient control over personal information. This shift reinforces the security protocols and empowers patients, making them active participants in managing their health data.

The potential of blockchain extends beyond data security and privacy to include facilitating health information exchanges. In the current healthcare landscape, the exchange of patient information between providers often encounters inefficiencies and security challenges, primarily due to disparate systems that need to communicate more effectively. Blockchain can provide a unified and secure platform to streamline these exchanges. Acting as a single source of truth ensures that all parties have access to the same, unalterable patient data. This technology can reduce, if not eliminate, the redundancy of medical records across multiple providers, ensuring that every physician has access to a patient's complete and accurate medical history. This improves the quality of care and enhances operational efficiencies by reducing the time and resources spent on verifying and reconciling medical records from different sources.

Despite these significant advantages, implementing blockchain in healthcare comes with its challenges. Technical complexities remain a significant hurdle. Blockchain technology demands substantial computational power and sophisticated algorithms that can be resource-intensive. Integrating this technology into healthcare IT systems poses considerable technical challenges and requires substantial initial and ongoing investment.

Regulatory and adoption challenges are critical in integrating blockchain into healthcare systems. The healthcare industry is heavily regulated, and any new technology must comply with many privacy and security regulations. Ensuring that blockchain solutions meet these regulatory requirements is crucial but often challenging due to the novel nature of the technology. Moreover, the widespread adoption of blockchain in healthcare requires buy-in from multiple stakeholders, including healthcare providers, IT professionals, and policymakers. Each group has expectations and reservations about the technology, which must be addressed through comprehensive education and demonstration of value.

As we conclude the exploration of blockchain in healthcare, it's clear that while the technology harbors the potential to transform healthcare data management, the path forward is layered with technological and regulatory complexities. These challenges require innovative technical solutions and collaborative efforts among technology developers, healthcare professionals, and regulatory bodies. As we move forward, the successful integration of blockchain into healthcare will hinge on our ability to navigate these complexities, ensuring that the technology enhances the security and efficiency of healthcare data management and aligns with the broader goals of improving patient care and safeguarding patient data privacy.

In the next chapter, we'll explore how digital tools and technologies are being leveraged to improve individual patient care and enhance the operational efficiencies of healthcare institutions, continuing our deep dive into the transformative impact of technology in healthcare.

Chapter 9 Advocacy and Policy Change

Imagine standing at the forefront of a movement, a collective force rallying for pivotal shifts in healthcare policy. This is where advocacy transforms from mere discussion to dynamic action. This chapter delves into the core of grassroots organizing—a fundamental strategy where your voice and others can catalyze real change in the healthcare system.

9.1 Building a Movement for Healthcare Reform

Grassroots Organizing Principles

Grassroots organizing in healthcare reform is about igniting and harnessing community power to advocate for systemic change. It begins with identifying common issues that resonate deeply with individuals and communities affected by existing healthcare policies. The principle of inclusivity is paramount; a successful movement must represent the diverse voices and experiences of all those it aims to serve. This includes patients who have navigated the labyrinth of healthcare bureaucracy, healthcare professionals who confront systemic inefficiencies daily, and caregivers who advocate tirelessly for their loved ones.

Building a movement also requires strategic planning and clear, achievable goals. Whether the aim is to influence local health-care policy, advocate for national reforms, or raise awareness about healthcare rights, each objective needs to be clearly defined and communicated. Effective grassroots movements thrive on transparency and the trust of their members, making consistent and open communication a cornerstone of organiz-ing. Training and empowering volunteers with the necessary skills to advocate, organize, and mobilize effectively ensures sustained engagement and impact.

Successful Case Studies

Reflecting on successful advocacy campaigns provides invalu-able insights. Take, for example, the movement for mental health parity in the United States, culminating in the passage of the Mental Health Parity and Addiction Equity Act of 2008. This landmark legislation, which required insurance companies to provide equitable benefits for mental health and substance use treatments, was largely the result of relentless advocacy by grassroots organizations that highlighted disparities in healthcare treatment.

Another profound case is the HIV/AIDS advocacy movement, which transformed the disease from a death sentence into a man-ageable condition. Organizations like ACT UP (AIDS Coalition to Unleash Power) employed dramatic and impactful activism to draw attention to the crisis, significantly influencing drug approval processes and pricing. These movements illustrate how sustained advocacy and community mobilization can lead to substantial policy changes that directly benefit millions of lives.

Engaging Stakeholders

For a grassroots movement to be effective, it must engage a broad spectrum of stakeholders. This includes forging alliances with healthcare professionals who can provide credibility and an in-depth understanding of the intricacies of healthcare policies. Engaging policymakers directly through lobbying efforts, public forums, and policy drafts is crucial in translating grassroots activism into tangible changes. It's also essential to involve patients and the general public—as the beneficiaries of policy changes and as active participants in the advocacy process. Their real-life experiences and testimonials can be powerful tools in shaping public opinion and policy.

Leveraging Social Media

In today's digital age, social media is a pivotal tool for advocacy. Platforms like Twitter, Facebook, and Instagram offer expansive reach and the ability to share information quickly and widely. Social media can mobilize supporters, coordinate actions, and sustain dialogue on critical issues. It allows for the viral spread of information, making it possible to bring national and international attention to local issues. For instance, the #MeToo movement, though broader than healthcare, exemplifies how social media can amplify voices, spread stories, and challenge systemic injustices. In the context of healthcare reform, social media campaigns can highlight disparities, advocate for policy changes, and keep followers engaged and informed about the progress and impacts of the advocacy efforts.

Through these discussions, it becomes evident that building a movement for healthcare reform is not just about rallying cries and public demonstrations; it's about strategic actions, inclusive community engagement, and the effective use of modern communication tools to advocate for change. By understanding and employing these principles, you can contribute to a movement that voices concerns and enacts substantial and lasting reforms in the healthcare system.

9.2 Lobbying for Health: Turning the Tables

Lobbying, often viewed through political maneuvering, is fundamentally about advocating for changes or preserving policies that influence our daily lives, particularly in healthcare. Understanding how to navigate this process can empower you to shift healthcare policies in favor of public well-being effectively. At its core, lobbying involves directly engaging policymakers to inform and persuade them about the merits or drawbacks of specific legislative actions. For those new to this arena, it begins with identifying the key legislators whose committee assignments or voting records align with your healthcare advocacy goals. Establishing a clear and well-researched position on specific healthcare issues, such as the need for improved patient rights or more accessible mental health services, forms the foundation of effective lobbying.

Equally important is the ability to communicate these positions clearly and compellingly. This involves presenting factual data and research and sharing compelling personal stories that highlight the human impact of existing policies. For instance, if advocating for expanded mental health coverage, bringing forward narratives of individuals whose lives could dramatically improve with better access to mental health services can be a powerful persuasion tool. These stories humanize the statistical data and create emotional resonance with policymakers, often catalyzing them into action. It's about making the issue real and urgent for those in the position to make a difference.

To support these efforts, numerous resources and training programs are available that can enhance your skills as a health-care lobbyist. Organizations like the American Association of Healthcare Administrative Management often conduct work-shops and seminars that provide insights into the legislative process, effective communication techniques, and strategies for successful lobbying. Additionally, many nonprofit advocacy groups offer resources that help you understand the legal and ethical aspects of lobbying. These training opportunities are invaluable for equipping yourself with the knowledge and skills needed to navigate the complex landscape of healthcare policy and effectively advocate for change.

Ethical Lobbying

Maintaining ethical integrity in lobbying is crucial. Ethical lobbying is grounded in transparency, honesty, and respect for the legislative process. This means ensuring that all interactions with policymakers are based on factual, verifiable information and that the motives behind your advocacy are clear and aimed at improving public health outcomes rather than personal gain. Ethical lobbying involves pursuing policies that are in the community's best interest, particularly for those who may need the voice or means to advocate for themselves. For instance, when lobbying for policies affecting lower-income populations' access to healthcare, it is vital to accurately and responsibly represent their needs and challenges accurately and responsibly.

A cornerstone of ethical lobbying is also the readiness to present the benefits and any potential drawbacks of proposed policy changes. This balanced approach not only aids policymakers in making informed decisions but also builds credibility and trustworthiness as a resource. Moreover, ethical lobbying involves listening to and respecting opposing viewpoints and fostering mutual respect and open dialogue, which is essential for finding sustainable solutions to complex healthcare issues.

Case Studies of Effective Lobbying

Examining case studies where effective lobbying led to significant policy changes can provide practical insights and inspiration. For example, the lobbying efforts that led to enacting the Children's Health Insurance Program (CHIP) in 1997 are a powerful example of how persistent and well-coordinated advocacy efforts can result in substantial legislative outcomes. CHIP has since provided millions of children in low-income families access to essential healthcare services, dramatically

85

improving health outcomes for a vulnerable population segment. This success was achieved through relentless advocacy by healthcare professionals, parents, and a broad coalition of stakeholders who unified their voices to highlight the critical need for pediatric healthcare coverage.

Another illustrative case is the lobbying done by patient advocacy groups to pass the 21st Century Cures Act in 2016. This comprehensive legislation, which aimed to accelerate drug development and bring new innovations and advances to patients who need them faster and more efficiently, was heavily influenced by lobbyists advocating for expanded funding for medical research and modification of the drug approval process at the FDA. These lobbyists effectively communicated the potential benefits of the act in terms of healthcare innovation and improving patient access to new therapies and treatments, showcasing the profound impact of well-strategized advocacy efforts.

You can significantly influence healthcare policy by understanding and engaging in the lobbying process, harnessing available training resources, and maintaining a commitment to ethical advocacy. Through dedicated efforts, it is possible to transform the healthcare landscape, ensuring policies that promote better health outcomes and equitable access to medical services for all individuals. As we continue to explore the power of advocacy in the next sections, remember that each step taken towards effective lobbying is a step towards a healthier society.

9.3 The Power of the Patient Voice in Media

The influence of traditional and new media in shaping public opinion and policy cannot be overstated. As an advocate for healthcare reform, harnessing this power through effective messaging is critical. Crafting resonate messages requires a deep understanding of the issues at hand and the ability to articulate these concerns in ways that connect with a broad audience. Begin by focusing on the core issues you understand best and can speak about with authority. Whether it's the need for better mental health services or equitable healthcare access, your message should be clear and concise, distilling complex problems into relatable impacts. For instance, rather than delving into intricate policy details, you might highlight how specific changes in legislation could prevent thousands of avoidable deaths annually, thereby humanizing and scaling the issue for your audience.

Furthermore, consider the emotional and logical appeals that will resonate most strongly with your intended audience when crafting your message. Emotional appeals can be powerful motivators, particularly when they involve personal stories or testimonials that exemplify broader issues. These narratives make the stakes clear and foster a personal connection with the audience, making the abstract tangibly urgent. On the other hand, logical appeals, supported by data and facts, reinforce the credibility of your message, providing the rational basis for why change is necessary. Balancing these approaches will enhance the impact of your communications, making them more compelling and persuasive.

Engaging effectively with the media requires a proactive strategy. While more immediate than digital platforms, traditional media outlets, television, radio, and newspapers, still wield significant influence, especially among certain demographics. Writing op-eds, participating in interviews, and being part of panel discussions are excellent ways to reach these audiences. Each of these formats offers different strengths: op-eds allow for detailed arguments and the opportunity to directly address misconceptions or counterarguments, while interviews and discussions provide a platform for personal charisma and immediacy, which can be very persuasive.

For newer media platforms, particularly social media, the strategies differ slightly due to the nature of the medium. Social media's strength lies in its ability to disseminate information quickly and interactively. It allows for real-time engagement with your audience, enabling immediate feedback and fostering a sense of community and dialogue. When using platforms like Twitter, Facebook, or Instagram, it is crucial to post regularly and engage with supporters and skeptics respectfully and informally. Additionally, using videos and infographics can significantly increase the engagement levels of your posts, as these formats are more likely to be shared, increasing the reach of your message.

Building productive relationships with journalists and media outlets is another critical strategy. Start by identifying reporters who cover healthcare or related topics and reach out with well-prepared pitches that include key facts and why the story matters. Being a reliable source is essential to being accessible, providing clear and timely information, and respecting journalistic deadlines. Building trust with journalists means they are more likely to come to you for insights or to clarify healthcare issues, providing more opportunities to influence public discourse.

Monitoring media coverage is essential to understanding how healthcare issues are being discussed publicly and responding effectively to misinformation or opposition. Tools like Google Alerts can notify you when specific terms are mentioned online, helping you keep track of emerging narratives. Responding to these mentions allows you to correct inaccuracies swiftly and reinforce positive messaging, maintaining control over the narrative.

In utilizing these strategies, you are not just sharing information but actively shaping the healthcare discourse. By effectively crafting messages, engaging with media, and building productive relationships, you elevate the patient's voice, turning personal stories and professional insights into powerful catalysts for change. This strategic approach amplifies your advocacy efforts and ensures that the narrative around healthcare reform is grounded in the real experiences and needs of those it aims to serve. As we transition from discussing media strategies, the next chapter will explore how technological advancements further transform patient care, providing new tools and platforms for advocacy and engagement in healthcare.

Chapter 10 The Mental Health Maze

Imagine you're standing in front of a vast, intricate network of pathways, each twist and turn representing different aspects of mental health care. As you navigate this labyrinth, one path— lined with pills and prescriptions—seems well-trodden, almost inviting. Yet, as familiar as this route appears, it's fraught with potential pitfalls and obscured corners. This is the mental health maze, a complex system where the reliance on psychiatric medications often overshadows more holistic approaches to wellness. In this chapter, we delve deep into this problem, exploring the nuances of psychiatric medications, their impacts, and the vital alternatives that offer a more rounded approach to mental health care.

10.1 Psychiatry's Pill Problem: A Critical Look

Over-reliance on Medications

The modern psychiatric landscape is, in many ways, dominated by a pharmacological approach to treatment. Medications like antidepressants, antipsychotics, and anxiolytics are often the first line of defense in managing mental health disorders. While these medications can be life-saving for many, their prevalent use raises crucial questions about the mental health system's dependency on them. For countless individuals, a prescription becomes a primary solution, sometimes at the expense of exploring underlying issues or integrating other therapeutic approaches. This over-reliance can lead to a kind of tunnel vision, where the potential for holistic treatment— including psychotherapy, lifestyle modifications, and community support—is overshadowed by the convenience of a pill.

The implications of this trend are profound. In settings where healthcare providers face time constraints or lack resources, prescribing medication becomes a quicker, more scalable option than long-term counseling or therapy. Moreover, the influence of pharmaceutical companies, which often promote the efficacy and benefits of their products, can also skew treatment practices towards medication. This environment creates a cycle where medications are not only normalized but also expected by patients seeking quick relief from distressing symptoms.

Side Effects and Long-term Impact

While psychiatric medications can be effective, their side effects and long-term impacts are considerable and warrant careful consideration. Common side effects range from mild—such as nausea and headaches—to more severe, including weight gain, sexual dysfunction, and increased risk of diabetes. Antipsychotics, for example, are associated with a notable risk of metabolic syndrome, which can lead to significant health complications over time.

The long-term impacts are perhaps even more concerning. Some individuals on long-term psychiatric medication may experience a blunting of emotions or difficulty engaging fully with life, a state sometimes referred to as "emotional anesthesia." Additionally, the discontinuation of these medications can lead to withdrawal symptoms that can be severe and debilitating, complicating the process of medication management and often leading to a dependency that can be hard to break.

Alternatives to Medication

Recognizing the limitations and risks associated with an over-reliance on medications, it is crucial to consider and develop non-pharmaceutical approaches to mental health care. Psychotherapy, for instance, offers a robust alternative, providing tools and strategies to manage mental health issues without the side effects associated with medications. Techniques such as Cognitive Behavioral Therapy (CBT), Dialectical Behavior Therapy (DBT), and others have been proven effective in treating a variety of mental health conditions, from depression and anxiety to more complex disorders like PTSD and borderline personality disorder.

Lifestyle changes also play a critical role in managing mental health. Regular physical activity, a balanced diet, adequate sleep, and mindfulness practices like meditation can significantly affect mental well-being. Additionally, community support—from peer support groups to community mental health services—can provide a network of assistance and understanding that strengthens the individual's coping mechanisms.

Reforming Prescription Practices

Significant reforms in prescription practices are necessary to address the challenges posed by the current over-reliance on medications. These reforms should focus on establishing a more integrated approach to mental health care, where medications are used judiciously and in conjunction with other therapeutic modalities. Educating healthcare providers about the full spectrum of mental health treatments and encouraging a culture where medications are not seen as the first or only solution is essential.

Moreover, policies that promote and fund alternative treatment options alleviate the pressure to default to pharmacological solutions. Insurance companies, for instance, should be encouraged to cover a broader range of therapies, making these options more accessible to a wider population. By broadening the scope of covered treatments, the mental health care system can provide more balanced, patient-centered care that truly addresses the diverse needs of those it serves.

Understanding the complex interplay between medications, their effects, and the viable alternatives available is crucial to navigating the mental health maze. By broadening our perspective and advocating for a more integrated approach to mental health care, we can ensure that treatment is effective, holistic, and responsive to each individual's needs.

10.2 Breaking Barriers: Access to Mental Health Care

Insurance Coverage Gaps

Navigating mental health care can often feel like trying to piece together a puzzle where several pieces are missing. These missing pieces frequently manifest as gaps in insurance coverage, which leave many individuals without the necessary access to mental health services. In many cases, insurance policies segregate mental health services from other medical services, often enforcing stricter limitations or higher co-pays. For some, even those with insurance, the coverage for mental health therapy sessions, psychiatrist visits, or even in-patient mental health services can be severely limited or excluded altogether. This disparity not only reflects an archaic separation of mind and body in healthcare but also perpetuates the struggle for individuals seeking mental health support, leaving them to bear the brunt of high out-of-pocket costs. For others, particularly in lower-income brackets, the high cost of mental health care without sufficient insurance coverage may altogether deter them from seeking necessary help. The ripple effects of these coverage gaps can be profound, leading to untreated mental health conditions that escalate into more severe, often more costly health crises that could have been prevented with earlier intervention.

One deeply affected group includes young adults, particularly those transitioning from family insurance plans or student health services. This transitional phase often leaves gaps in their mental health care during a critical period of their lives when many severe mental health conditions tend to manifest. Moreover, the inconsistency in Medicaid expansion across states under the Affordable Care Act has created a patchwork of coverage that disproportionately affects the most vulnerable populations, exacerbating regional disparities in access to mental health services. Addressing these gaps requires a multifaceted approach, beginning with policy reforms to standardize and expand mental health coverage to be truly inclusive and accessible. Insurance companies must be held accountable, ensuring parity in coverage for mental and physical health care, thereby reducing the financial barriers preventing so many from seeking help.

Stigma and Cultural Barriers

Beyond the systemic barriers posed by insurance, cultural and social stigmas surrounding mental health significantly hinder individuals from accessing care. Despite growing awareness and advocacy, mental health still carries a heavy stigma in many communities, often seen as a weakness or a fault of character rather than a treatable health condition. This pervasive stigma can dissuade individuals from seeking help for fear of judgment or ostracization from their community. For some cultures, mental health issues are not acknowledged as legitimate health problems, and discussing them openly might be considered taboo. This cultural imprint can lead to a significant underutilization of available mental health resources, as individuals may opt to suffer in silence rather than face the stigma associated with these conditions.

Efforts to dismantle these barriers must include community-

based education initiatives that promote mental health awareness and reshape public perceptions. Schools, workplaces, and
religious institutions can play pivotal roles in this educational
outreach, providing platforms to challenge myths and educate
individuals about the signs and symptoms of mental health
issues and the importance of seeking assistance. Real-life
stories from individuals who have navigated these challenges
and found support can also be influential in changing hearts and
minds, making mental health discussions more relatable and
less intimidating.

Telehealth as a Solution

In the quest to bridge the gap in mental health services, telehealth has emerged as a pivotal tool, particularly in reaching
underserved or remote areas. Telehealth, or telemedicine,
involves delivering health services via telecommunications
technologies, such as video calls, phone consultations, or mobile
health applications. For mental health, telehealth has proven
exceptionally effective, allowing individuals to receive therapy
and counseling in the privacy and comfort of their own homes.
This method not only circumvents the logistical barriers of
traditional face-to-face sessions, such as transportation or
scheduling conflicts but also provides a level of anonymity that
can ease the discomfort associated with seeking mental health
care.

Moreover, telehealth has the potential to reach individuals in
rural or isolated communities who previously had limited or
no access to mental health professionals. By connecting these
individuals with therapists and mental health resources via the

internet or mobile networks, telehealth helps to democratize access to mental health care. However, expanding telehealth services must be accompanied by efforts to ensure these digital solutions are accessible to all, including addressing the digital divide that prevents many from accessing these technologies. Investments in broadband infrastructure, particularly in rural areas, and programs to provide necessary technologies to low-income households are essential to making telehealth a viable solution for all.

Policy Changes for Better Access

Comprehensive policy changes are necessary to revolutionize access to mental health care. These changes aim not only to eliminate the insurance coverage gaps and cultural barriers that stifle access but also to integrate and prioritize mental health care as a fundamental part of overall health care. Policies need to enforce mental health parity laws more rigorously, ensuring that insurance coverage for mental health services is on par with that for physical health services. Additionally, legislation could incentivize providers to adopt and expand telehealth services through funding and grants, making these technologies more widespread and integrated into traditional healthcare systems.

Moreover, policies that foster an inclusive approach to mental health acknowledging and addressing the specific needs of diverse cultural and socio-economic groups, can help to mitigate the stigma and accessibility issues that currently plague the system. By implementing these changes, the hope is to construct a mental health care system that is not only more accessible but also more compassionate, responsive, and effective in meeting the needs of all individuals.

10.3 Alternative Approaches to Mental Wellness

Exploring mental wellness extends beyond conventional medical treatments and delves into various evidence-based alternative approaches that can significantly enhance mental health. Among these, mindfulness and meditation have emerged as powerful tools that foster a deep sense of mental clarity and peace. Extensive research supports the effectiveness of mindfulness practices in reducing symptoms of anxiety, depression, and stress. These practices involve a focused awareness of the present moment, encouraging individuals to observe their thoughts and feelings without judgment. Meditation, a complementary practice, often involves guided imagery or breathing exercises that help to calm the mind and align the body and spirit. The beauty of these techniques lies in their simplicity and accessibility, enabling anyone to practice them without the need for specialized equipment or even much space.

Physical activity is another cornerstone of mental wellness that is universally acknowledged for its profound benefits on mental health. Regular physical exercise, be it yoga, walking, or more vigorous activities like cycling or swimming, releases endorphins—often referred to as the body's natural antidepressants. But the benefits extend beyond biochemical; physical activity provides a structured routine, a distraction from negative thoughts, and can improve self-esteem by achieving fitness goals. The inclusivity of physical activity makes it a viable option for a wide range of individuals, regardless of age or fitness level, underscoring its role as an essential component of a holistic approach to mental wellness.

Incorporating traditional and cultural practices into mental health treatment offers another layer of personalization and effectiveness, particularly for individuals from diverse cultural backgrounds. Traditional practices such as acupuncture, Ayurveda, or even spiritual rituals like smudging can play significant roles in the mental wellness strategies of many communities. These practices often carry centuries of history and a deep spiritual significance that can enhance their therapeutic effect. For many, these traditional methods are not just about treating symptoms but are integral to their way of life and worldview, providing comfort and familiarity which can be particularly soothing during times of mental distress.

Community support systems represent a vital aspect of promoting mental wellness and recovery. The power of community in mental health care cannot be overstated; support groups, whether online or in person, provide a platform for sharing experiences, offering and receiving advice, and simply feeling understood and not alone. Community centers, religious organizations, and even online forums can serve as pillars of support, offering activities and resources that promote mental health. These systems not only help reduce the stigma associated with mental health issues but also empower individuals by connecting them with others who can provide encouragement and understanding.

Challenges in Adoption

While the benefits of these alternative approaches to mental wellness are clear, their integration into mainstream mental health systems is not without challenges. One significant barrier is the prevailing skepticism within some medical communities, where a strong preference for traditional pharmacological treatments often persists. Overcoming this skepticism requires continuous education and communication about the benefits and validity of alternative methods supported by scientific research.

Another hurdle is the need for widespread professional training in these alternative practices, which can prevent healthcare providers from recommending them to patients. Expanding the curriculum in medical training institutions to include alternative wellness methods could help bridge this gap. Additionally, insurance coverage for alternative treatments is often limited, making them inaccessible to those who need help to afford to pay out of pocket. Advocating for insurance policies that recognize and cover a broader range of treatments could play a crucial role in their adoption and widespread use.

As we close this exploration of alternative approaches to mental wellness, we reflect on the rich tapestry of options available that go beyond traditional medication. Each approach offers unique benefits and, when integrated thoughtfully into treatment plans, can provide a more comprehensive path to mental health that respects individual preferences and cultural backgrounds. This holistic view enhances individual well-being and enriches the collective approach to mental health care.

Continuing into the next chapter, we will delve into the critical topic of women's health within the healthcare industry, exploring the unique challenges and advances in this vital area. Here, we aim to shed light on disparities, advocate for equitable health solutions, and celebrate the strides made towards global understanding and improving women's health.

12

Chapter 11 Women's Health in the Healthcare Industry

Imagine walking into a room filled with the latest medical technology and treatments designed to ensure health and longevity. Now imagine realizing that much of this innovation is based on research that predominantly studied only half of the population—excluding or underrepresenting the other half based solely on gender. This is not a fictional scenario but a historical reality in the realm of medical research where women, constituting half of the global population, have been significantly underrepresented. This chapter delves into the gender gap within medical research, its profound implications on women's health care, and the ongoing efforts to rectify this longstanding oversight.

11.1 The Gender Gap in Medical Research

Historical Exclusion

The exclusion of women from clinical studies and medical research traces back to various scientific and socio-cultural factors that have historically viewed the male body as the default model. For decades, researchers justified the exclusion of women from studies due to hormonal variations and potential pregnancy complications, which they argued could skew results. Such exclusion has resulted in a troubling knowledge gap, with many medications and treatments being less effective, or sometimes even harmful, for women. This oversight was highlighted in the late 20th century, which saw a push towards rectifying these disparities, culminating in policy changes such as the NIH Revitalization Act of 1993 that required federally funded clinical research to include women.

Bias in Treatment

The repercussions of this historical exclusion are evident in the present-day bias in treatment and diagnosis across various medical disciplines. Cardiovascular disease serves as a poignant example. Traditionally considered a man's disease, cardiovascular research predominantly focused on male subjects, leading to a diagnostic and treatment framework that fails to adequately address the pathophysiology and presentation of the disease in women. Women are more likely to have atypical symptoms and thus are often underdiagnosed and undertreated. This bias extends beyond misdiagnosis and affects the efficacy of drugs and treatment protocols, which may not have been adequately tested on female subjects.

Efforts to Bridge the Gap

In recent decades, a concerted effort has been made to bridge this gender gap in medical research. Initiatives like the Women's Health Research Institute at Northwestern University have been pivotal in advocating for the inclusion of sex as a biological variable in all stages of research, from pre-clinical trials to clinical settings. Funding agencies have also begun to enforce more stringent requirements for including female subjects in research studies. However, challenges persist, notably in the field of mental health and pharmacology, where sex-based differences in responses to drugs and therapies are still underexplored. The complexity of these challenges is deepened by the intersectionality of gender with race, ethnicity, and socioeconomic status, which also need to be considered to address the disparities in health outcomes fully.

Advocating for Equity

Advocacy for gender equity in medical research and healthcare treatment requires a multifaceted approach. Advocacy must aim to increase female participation in clinical trials and ensure that research questions are designed to address specific women's health issues. Policy advocacy is crucial here—supporting legislation that promotes comprehensive and inclusive health research and ensures that findings are translated into practice. Additionally, educational initiatives targeting both the public and healthcare providers can raise awareness about the importance of gender-specific medical research and encourage advocacy for equitable healthcare.

As we continue to explore and address these critical issues, it becomes increasingly clear that the path to equitable healthcare is through rigorous, inclusive, and diversified medical research that recognizes and values every patient's differences.

11.2 Navigating Reproductive Health

Access to comprehensive reproductive health services is a fundamental aspect of women's healthcare. Yet, many women face many barriers that impede their ability to receive the care they need. These obstacles are not just medical or logistical but often extend into legal, financial, and geographic realms, creating a complex web that can discourage or outright prevent women from accessing vital services. Legal barriers, for instance, manifest through restrictive laws and policies that limit access to services like contraception and abortion. These laws can vary significantly by region, leaving women in some areas with far fewer healthcare options than those in more permissive environments. Financial obstacles are similarly formidable. Despite some legislative efforts to improve affordability, many women find themselves without the necessary insurance coverage or financial resources to cover the costs of essential reproductive health services. This situation is further exacerbated for low-income women who may lack the means to travel to facilities that offer the needed services, underscoring the intertwined nature of financial and geographic barriers.

The imperative for comprehensive reproductive health education cannot be overstated. Education informs women of their healthcare options and empowers them to make knowledgeable decisions about their health. Yet, the current state of reproductive health education is often fragmented and variably accessible. Many women receive incomplete information, which can lead to misconceptions and anxiety regarding reproductive health choices. Comprehensive education should encompass the biological aspects of reproductive health and practical information on accessing services, understanding rights, and navigating the healthcare system effectively. Such education must be inclusive, culturally sensitive, and tailored to reach women of all ages and backgrounds, ensuring that every woman has the tools to manage her reproductive health proactively.

Policies play a pivotal role in shaping access to reproductive health services. Current policies vary widely, with some supporting broad access to reproductive healthcare while others impose stringent restrictions that can limit or deny access to essential services. To improve access to reproductive health services, policy changes must focus on removing unnecessary barriers and supporting women's health choices. Proposed changes could include expanding insurance coverage to include all aspects of reproductive healthcare, increasing funding for reproductive health services to ensure broader access, and enacting laws that protect against discrimination based on reproductive choices. By aligning policies with the needs and rights of women, lawmakers and health professionals can enhance the quality and accessibility of reproductive healthcare, ensuring that women have the support they need to make informed decisions.

Support systems play a crucial role in reproductive healthcare, providing women with the resources and emotional support necessary to navigate their health choices confidently. These systems can include counseling services, which offer guidance and support for women making difficult health decisions, or community services that provide practical assistance, such as transportation to medical appointments or financial aid for healthcare costs. The strengthening of these support systems is vital. They assist women in accessing the care they need and create a network of support that can help them feel less isolated in their healthcare journeys. Enhancing these services, ensuring they are accessible and responsive to the needs of diverse communities of women, can transform the landscape of reproductive healthcare, making it more inclusive and support-ive of every woman's health needs.

11.3 Empowering Women to Advocate for Their Health

Empowering women to advocate for their health within the healthcare system is pivotal in addressing their unique chal-lenges. Self-advocacy is not merely about speaking up; it's about being informed, confident, and assertive in navigating a system that has not always recognized their specific health needs. One effective strategy for self-advocacy is education. Women equipped with comprehensive knowledge about their health conditions are more likely to engage actively in their care decisions. This involves understanding potential treatment options, the side effects of prescribed medications, and the right questions to ask during medical consultations. Furthermore, women should be encouraged to maintain detailed health records, including test results and treatment histories, which can be invaluable during medical appointments and when seeking second opinions.

Navigating the healthcare system effectively also requires identifying and choosing gender-sensitive healthcare providers who are not only skilled but also empathetic to women's health issues. This search can begin with recommendations from trusted sources such as family, friends, or patient advocacy groups. Online platforms and forums can also provide reviews and testimonials about healthcare providers, which can be crucial in making informed decisions. Once a potential healthcare provider is found, preparing for the initial visit is essential. Women should feel empowered to discuss openly their health concerns without feeling rushed or dismissed. Creating a list of symptoms, concerns, and questions before appointments can help maximize the time spent with healthcare providers and foster a more productive dialogue.

Building a robust support network is another crucial aspect of empowering women in their health advocacy efforts. These networks can include family members, friends, support groups, and online communities that provide emotional support, share experiences, and offer practical advice. Especially for chronic conditions, these networks can be lifelines that give encouragement and understanding. Additionally, professional networks, such as patient advocates or social workers, can offer guidance on navigating complex healthcare systems and accessing necessary services. These professionals can assist in understanding patient rights, which is crucial for advocating effectively within the healthcare system.

Policy advocacy presents a powerful avenue for driving systemic change in women's healthcare. Women can engage in policy advocacy by participating in public forums, connecting with policymakers, or joining advocacy groups focusing on women's health issues. Writing letters, making calls, or scheduling meetings with legislators to discuss women's health concerns can influence healthcare policies. Furthermore, participation in health policy workshops or seminars can provide insights into the legislative process and effective advocacy strategies, equipping women with the tools needed to advocate for meaningful change at the systemic level.

In fostering an environment where women are empowered to advocate for their health, we address individual health needs and contribute to the broader goal of achieving gender equity in healthcare. This empowerment aids in dismantling the barriers that have historically prevented women from receiving appropriate and effective healthcare, ensuring that future generations of women have better health outcomes and a more equitable healthcare experience.

As this chapter concludes, we reflect on the empowering strategies that equip women to navigate and influence the healthcare system effectively. From developing self-advocacy skills and building supportive networks to engaging in policy advocacy, the tools discussed here are essential for fostering a healthcare environment that acknowledges and addresses the unique needs of women. These efforts are not just about improving individual health outcomes—they're about transforming the healthcare landscape into truly inclusive and equitable. As we continue to explore the complexities of healthcare, the next chapter will delve into the opioid crisis, examining its roots, impacts, and essential strategies for recovery and prevention.

13

Chapter 12 The Opioid Crisis: A Systemic Failure

In the quiet corners of suburban America, a storm has been brewing, insidiously woven its way into the fabric of everyday life. Imagine a scenario where what begins as a routine dental extraction or a treatment for minor back pain spirals into a harrowing dependency on pain-relieving drugs. This grim picture paints only a fraction of the reality many face in the current opioid crisis—a crisis not born out of the dark alleys of illicit drug trade but from the well-lit corridors of medical institutions and the boardrooms of some of the nation's most trusted pharmaceutical companies. Here lies a tale of individual tragedy and systemic failure, where the intertwining of profit-driven motives and inadequate regulatory oversight turned a medical solution into a national nightmare.

12.1 The Making of an Epidemic: Pharmaceutical Companies and Opioids

Marketing Misconduct

The opioid epidemic, as you might already discern, didn't start in the shadows but in the aggressive marketing strategies of pharmaceutical giants. Companies like Purdue Pharma, the maker of OxyContin, embarked on a massive campaign in the late 1990s and early 2000s, promoting opioids as a safe and effective solution to chronic pain. These campaigns massively downplayed the risk of addiction, a critical detail that was obscured under the glossy sheen of marketing brochures and persuasive sales pitches. Sales representatives were incentivized with hefty bonuses to push opioids into every possible market, from dentists for minor dental work to general practitioners for common complaints like back pain. The narrative sold was compelling: opioids were portrayed as a humanitarian answer to the problem of chronic pain, a narrative eagerly embraced by healthcare providers and patients alike.

Regulatory Failures

While pharmaceutical companies pushed opioids into the market with zeal, regulatory bodies like the FDA played a less than stellar role in curbing this enthusiasm. The approval of OxyContin in 1995 without adequate evidence about its safety over long periods is a glaring example. The FDA's oversight mechanisms missed misleading claims made by opioid manufacturers, which under-reported the addictive potentials of their products. This lapse was not merely an oversight but a catastrophic failure, considering the FDA's role as the guardian of public health. The regulatory frameworks that were supposed to act as checks and balances were instead mired in bureaucracy and, in some cases, swayed by the very industry they were meant to regulate—a phenomenon known as regulatory capture.

Holding Companies Accountable

The legal and financial ramifications for the companies responsible for fueling the opioid crisis have been substantial, yet many argue that they are not significant enough. In recent years, companies like Purdue Pharma have faced multiple lawsuits from states and municipalities claiming billions in damages for the social and medical costs incurred by opioid addiction. These legal battles culminated in Purdue filing for bankruptcy in 2019 as part of an agreement to settle thousands of lawsuits. However, for many, these actions are too little, too late. The settlements, while providing financial compensation, do little to undo the immense social damage or address the ongoing dependency issues faced by thousands of individuals. The call for holding these companies accountable remains a contentious issue, with ongoing debates about the role of punitive damages versus more significant regulatory reforms to prevent future crises.

Lessons Learned

Reflecting on the opioid crisis offers crucial lessons in pharmaceutical regulation and healthcare practices. First, it underscores the importance of rigorous, evidence-based drug approval processes that thoroughly assess both the efficacy and risks of new medications. Secondly, it highlights the critical need for ongoing monitoring of drug effects post-market. This area had been grossly neglected, allowing opioid addiction rates to skyrocket before significant regulatory actions were taken. Finally, this crisis has catalyzed a broader discourse on pain management, emphasizing the need for comprehensive approaches that include non-pharmacological options, thus hopefully preventing the over-reliance on pharmaceutical solutions seen in the past.

In exploring these dimensions of the opioid crisis, we confront uncomfortable truths about the intersections of healthcare, regulation, and corporate profit. This scenario invites not just passive observation but active engagement and advocacy for better standards and practices that prioritize patient well-being over corporate profits. As we continue to unravel the layers, we hope to foster a healthcare landscape that truly upholds the principles of care and ethical responsibility.

12.2 Pain Management: Alternatives and Solutions

In the vast realm of healthcare, managing pain without the crutch of opioids is not just a necessity but a movement towards a more sustainable and patient-focused approach to healing. As we steer away from opioid dependency, a variety of non-opioid pain management strategies have come to the forefront, offering relief without the dangerous side effects associated with opioids. Physical therapy, for instance, stands as a cornerstone in this alternative pain management paradigm. Unlike quick-fix solutions, physical therapy addresses the root causes of pain through a customized regimen of exercises and manual therapy techniques aimed at improving mobility, strengthening muscles, and alleviating pain through physical rehabilitation. It's a proactive approach that relieves pain and enhances bodily function, potentially reducing the risk of injury and pain recurrence.

Similarly, acupuncture, an ancient practice rooted in traditional Chinese medicine, has gained significant traction and acceptance in Western pain management strategies. By stimulating specific points on the body with thin needles, acupuncture seeks to restore balance and flow in the body's energy, offering a unique mechanism to alleviate pain. Clinical studies have shown that acupuncture can be particularly effective in treating chronic pain conditions such as arthritis, lower back pain, and migraines. It offers a stark contrast to opioid treatments by providing a non-invasive solution that facilitates the body's natural healing processes and offers relief without the risks of addiction or overdose.

Moreover, the development and utilization of non-addictive medications have opened new doors for pain management. Medications such as NSAIDs (non-steroidal anti-inflammatory drugs) and certain antidepressants are now regularly prescribed as effective treatments for pain, offering significant relief without the addictive properties of opioids. These medications, while not entirely devoid of side effects, present a significantly lower risk profile compared to opioids, making them a safer choice for long-term pain management.

The role of patient education in this context cannot be over-stated. Understanding the available pain management options and the potential risks and benefits of each is crucial for patients. Educated patients are more likely to have realistic expectations and make informed decisions about pain management strate-gies. Healthcare providers must, therefore, prioritize patient education, discussing not only the details of each treatment option but also lifestyle changes and self-care practices that can help manage pain. This education should also include strategies for safely using prescribed medications, recognizing signs of dependency, and understanding when to seek help, ensuring patients are well-prepared to manage their pain responsibly.

Integrative pain management programs represent another sig-nificant stride forward, offering tailored, patient-centered care that combines multiple therapeutic approaches. These programs typically involve a team of healthcare providers, including doctors, physical therapists, psychologists, and al-ternative medicine practitioners, who collaboratively create a comprehensive pain management plan. This multidisciplinary approach not only addresses the physical symptoms of pain but also the psychological aspects, often incorporating therapy and counseling to help patients cope with the emotional and mental stress associated with chronic pain. The benefits of such integrative programs are manifold; they not only improve pain management outcomes but also enhance patients' overall quality of life, fostering a sense of empowerment and control over their health.

Policy changes are imperative to support and expand these alternative pain management strategies. Legislation aimed at promoting the availability and affordability of physical therapy, acupuncture, and integrative pain management programs could drastically reduce the reliance on opioids. These policies could include increased funding for research into non-opioid pain treatments, insurance reforms to cover a broader range of pain management therapies, and education programs for healthcare providers to expand their knowledge and skills in applying these methods. By shifting policy focus from merely controlling opioid prescriptions to actively promoting alternative pain management solutions, we can create a healthcare environment that not only mitigates the risk of opioid dependency but also enhances the efficacy and accessibility of pain management treatments, paving the way for a healthier, more resilient population.

12.3 Healing Communities: Addressing the Aftermath of the Opioid Crisis

In the wake of the opioid epidemic, communities across the nation have been left grappling with the consequences of widespread addiction. The fabric of these communities, strained by loss and disruption, now faces the arduous task of healing and rebuilding. Central to these efforts are community-based recovery programs, which have emerged as beacons of hope and restoration. These programs vary widely in their approaches but share a common goal: to provide holistic support and recovery services tailored to the unique needs of individuals recovering from opioid addiction.

One notable approach within these programs is the emphasis on peer support—a method where individuals who are in recovery themselves act as mentors to those newly embarking on this path. This peer-to-peer model not only fosters a sense of understanding and empathy but also helps to break down the stigma associated with addiction, making it easier for individuals to seek help. Moreover, many of these programs integrate various therapeutic modalities, such as cognitive-behavioral therapy, art therapy, and family counseling, to address recovery's psychological and emotional dimensions. The success of these programs often lies in their community-centric approach, which cultivates a supportive network that reinforces the individual's journey toward recovery, thereby enhancing the resilience of the entire community.

Turning to broader public health strategies, it becomes clear that tackling the opioid crisis requires a multifaceted approach. One of the cornerstone strategies is harm reduction, which seeks to minimize the adverse health, social, and legal impacts associated with drug use without necessarily requiring abstinence. Harm reduction policies might include the provision of naloxone, a medication designed to reverse opioid overdose rapidly, or the establishment of supervised consumption sites where individuals can use opioids under medical supervision. These strategies are not without controversy; however, evidence suggests they play a crucial role in saving lives and reducing the spread of infections like HIV and hepatitis among drug-using populations.

Another pivotal element of public health strategy is enhancing the accessibility of treatment programs. Despite the growing need, many who suffer from opioid addiction do not receive the treatment they require. Barriers such as cost, lack of insurance coverage, and geographical constraints can prevent access to necessary services. Addressing these barriers means increasing funding for addiction treatment programs, expanding insurance coverage, and implementing mobile health clinics to serve remote or underserved areas. Furthermore, public education campaigns are essential to change public perceptions of addiction and increase awareness about the signs of opioid misuse and the available resources for help.

The impact of opioid addiction extends beyond the individual; it deeply affects families and communities, making support for families an integral part of the recovery process. Family counseling and support groups can provide the necessary tools for understanding addiction and learning how to support a loved one during recovery. These services help families navigate the complex emotions and challenges that arise from addiction, such as dealing with the stigma of addiction, understanding the risk of relapse, and rebuilding trust. Additionally, programs that offer educational resources about addiction can empower families with knowledge, reducing the sense of helplessness and fostering a proactive approach to recovery.

Building resilience in communities devastated by the opioid crisis involves a concerted effort to not only address the immediate impacts of addiction but also to lay the groundwork for long-term recovery and prevention. This includes investing in community resources such as education, job training, and affordable housing, which can alleviate some of the socioeconomic factors that contribute to substance abuse. Community centers, schools, and local organizations play a critical role in this regard, offering programs that promote healthy lifestyles, provide youth with constructive activities, and foster a sense of community cohesion.

As this chapter draws to a close, it is evident that healing the wounds inflicted by the opioid crisis requires a comprehensive approach that encompasses effective recovery programs, strategic public health policies, robust support systems for families, and initiatives aimed at building resilient communities. Each strategy, interwoven with the others, contributes to a fabric of recovery and hope—a renewed landscape where communities bounce back and thrive. As we transition from the challenges posed by opioids to the broader issues of healthcare accessibility discussed in the next chapter, it remains clear that the journey towards a healthier society is ongoing, demanding continuous commitment and adaptability.

14

Chapter 13 Health Literacy: Empowering Patients with Knowledge

Imagine sitting across from your doctor in a cold, sterile office, the walls echoing with the faint sounds of the bustling clinic outside. Your doctor is explaining the treatment options for your condition, but the jargon is dense, the options are complex, and the implications profound. Feeling overwhelmed, you nod along, not fully understanding the consequences of your choices. This scenario is far too common, reflecting a gap in health literacy that leaves many patients navigating their healthcare decisions through a fog of confusion. This chapter aims to clear that fog, empower you with the knowledge and strategies to understand and assert your rights within the healthcare system, and ensure you are an informed participant in your healthcare journey.

13.1 Understanding Your Rights as a Patient

Patient Rights Overview

Every patient entering the healthcare system is armed with rights designed to protect their dignity, privacy, and access to information—fundamental principles underpinning patient-centered care. These rights include but are not limited to, the right to informed consent, which ensures that you are fully educated about the risks and benefits of treatments before agreeing to them. The right to privacy under the Health Insurance Portability and Accountability Act (HIPAA) safeguards your personal health information, restricting how it can be shared and requiring your consent for most disclosures that aren't directly related to your care.

Understanding these rights is the first step in navigating the healthcare system more effectively. For instance, the right to informed consent is a critical aspect of patient care that requires doctors to provide clear and comprehensive information about treatment options. This means explaining the treatments in terms you can understand, outlining alternative options, and clearly stating the potential risks and benefits. By fully understanding the details of your treatment, you are better positioned to make decisions that align with your personal health goals and ethical beliefs.

Navigating Healthcare Legally

Navigating the healthcare system legally involves a clear understanding of the protections afforded to you under laws like HIPAA. HIPAA not only protects the privacy of your health information but also grants you the right to access your medical records, request corrections to your health information, and obtain a record of disclosures of your health information for purposes other than treatment, payment, or healthcare operations. Awareness of these rights can significantly enhance your ability to manage your health records and control your personal information.

Moreover, understanding these legal aspects helps when you need to challenge a healthcare decision or file a complaint. For instance, if you feel your rights under HIPAA have been violated—perhaps through unauthorized access to your medical records—you have the right to file a complaint with your provider's HIPAA Compliance Officer or directly with the U.S. Department of Health and Human Services.

Advocating for Your Needs

Advocating for your health needs is essential in ensuring that your rights are respected and that you receive the care you deserve. Effective communication is key in this advocacy. It involves being clear about your expectations, asking questions until you understand the implications of your care, and speaking up if you feel your rights are being overlooked. For example, if you are uncomfortable with the proposed medical treatment, you are entitled to ask for more information, seek a second opinion, or refuse treatment.

It's also important to document your interactions with healthcare providers. Keeping detailed records of your medical appointments, treatments, and any communications about your care can be invaluable, especially if discrepancies or issues arise. These records provide a clear trail of information that can support your position should you need to advocate for yourself in disputes or complaints.

Resources for Support

Several resources and organizations are available to help you navigate legal challenges and advocate effectively within the healthcare system. Organizations such as the Patient Advocate Foundation provide patients with mediation and arbitration services to resolve healthcare disputes. Additionally, local legal aid societies often offer free or low-cost advice on medical, legal issues, helping you understand your rights and the steps you can take to advocate for yourself.

In exploring patient rights and legal navigation within the healthcare system, we uncover the tools and knowledge you need to be an informed, confident advocate for your health. By understanding your rights, mastering the legal landscape, and harnessing effective advocacy strategies, you transform from a passive healthcare recipient into an active, empowered participant. This shift improves your personal healthcare outcomes and contributes to the broader goal of more transparent, equitable, and respectful healthcare for all.

13.2 Decoding Medical Bills and Insurance Statements

Navigating the labyrinth of healthcare billing is akin to decipher-ing a complex code filled with medical jargon, various charges, and often, little explanation. When you receive a medical bill or an insurance statement, it's essential to understand the various components that make up the total cost. Typically, these documents will list charges such as room fees if you've been hos-pitalized, costs for procedures performed, medication charges, and potentially ambiguous items labeled as 'miscellaneous' which can often be perplexing. Each of these entries corresponds to specific services or products provided during your medical care, and understanding these can help you verify whether the charges are accurate or if an error might have slipped through.

For instance, room fees can vary depending on the type of room you were assigned (private versus shared), and procedure costs can fluctuate based on the equipment and resources used. It's crucial to cross-reference these charges with the details of the care you received. Sometimes, discrepancies arise, such as being billed for medications you have yet to accept or procedures that were not performed. This is where a thorough review of your bill plays a critical role. By comparing your medical records and the detailed billing statement, you can identify any inconsistencies or mistakes that may have been made.

Disputing errors on medical bills and insurance statements is a meticulous process, but ensuring you only pay for the services you receive is necessary. Start by contacting your healthcare provider's billing department to discuss the charges you believe must be corrected. Having documentation on hand is beneficial, such as detailed notes from your hospital stay or records of the medications administered. Be clear and concise in your communication, and don't hesitate to ask for a detailed explanation of specific charges. If the billing department acknowledges the error, request a corrected bill and monitor your statements to ensure the adjustments are made.

However, if the resolution isn't straightforward and the health-care provider disputes the charges, it may be necessary to escalate the issue. This can involve contacting your health insurance company to contest a claim's denial or clarify coverage details. Often, insurance statements — known as Explanation of Benefits (EOB) — provide insights into what was covered under your insurance policy and what was not, and why. Understanding the terminology and the breakdown of covered versus non-covered charges, co-pays, deductibles, and co-insurance can be pivotal in identifying where errors might have occurred or what might have been processed incorrectly by your insurance.

Negotiating medical bills is another crucial aspect, especially if you find yourself facing correct but financially overwhelming charges. Many need to be made aware that medical costs can often be negotiated down, or payment plans can be arranged to ease the burden. Initiating these negotiations can be daunting, but starting the conversation is the first step. Approach the healthcare provider's billing office with your financial concerns. It's helpful to be honest about your financial situation and ask if there are options for reducing the charges or setting up a manageable payment plan. Medical facilities have financial assistance programs for which you might qualify. These programs can significantly reduce medical expenses and are particularly useful for large, unexpected medical bills.

Lastly, clarifying insurance coverage and benefits is essential for managing future healthcare interactions. Each insurance policy has specifics regarding what types of care and procedures are covered and to what extent. Familiarizing yourself with these details can prevent unexpected expenses in the future. You should review your insurance policy annually or after any major health incidents to better understand your coverage. This is also an opportunity to make adjustments to your plan during open enrollment periods to ensure your health insurance meets your current health needs.

In essence, becoming proficient in decoding medical bills and insurance statements equips you with the knowledge to protect yourself from overcharges and errors and better manage your healthcare finances. As you navigate these documents, remember that each line item tells part of your healthcare story, and you have the right to understand and question every charge you encounter.

13.3 The Role of Patient Advocacy Groups

In the vast and often intricate healthcare landscape, where navigating treatment options, insurance complexities, and legal rights can feel overwhelming, patient advocacy groups stand out as beacons of support, education, and empowerment. These organizations play a pivotal role in ensuring that patients do not face the healthcare journey alone but are equipped with knowledge, resources, and collective strength to advocate for their needs and rights.

Patient advocacy groups vary widely in their focus and operations, ranging from those offering support for specific diseases, such as the American Diabetes Association, to broader organizations like the Patient Advocate Foundation, which provides assistance across various conditions. These groups work tirelessly to ensure that patients and their families receive the necessary support to navigate the often daunting healthcare system. They offer educational resources that demystify medical terminology, explain patient rights, and provide information about treatment options. Moreover, they offer tools and support for direct advocacy, helping patients to communicate effectively with healthcare providers and insurance companies and to challenge decisions when necessary.

Finding the right advocacy group can significantly enhance your ability to manage your health condition and navigate the healthcare system more effectively. When searching for an advocacy group, it's crucial to consider the specificity of your health condition and the type of support you need. Start by researching online, where most reputable organizations have a presence. Look for groups that provide general information and offer resources tailored to specific conditions or demographics. Additionally, healthcare providers often recommend reputable advocacy groups that align with your health needs.

Once you have identified potential groups, evaluate their missions, programs, and the resources they offer. Many organizations will provide patient education, legal advocacy, or direct support services like help navigating insurance issues. It's also important to assess the community aspect of the group—whether it offers support networks, which can be invaluable in providing emotional support and practical advice from others who have faced similar challenges. Engaging with these groups often means actively participating in online forums and in-person meetings or advocacy events. These platforms allow you to gain information and support and share your experiences and insights, contributing to the community and enriching the support system.

The impact of patient advocacy groups on healthcare policy and individual patient care cannot be overstated. These groups have successfully influenced healthcare policies through collective action and lobbying to ensure more patient-friendly regulations. Their efforts have led to the enactment of laws that protect patient rights, improve access to care, and ensure fair treatment within the healthcare system. On an individual level, the empowerment and education provided by these groups enable patients to make informed decisions about their care, advocate effectively for their needs, and secure the best possible outcomes for their health situations.

As you consider engaging with a patient advocacy group, remember that your voice adds significant value to the collective effort to improve healthcare systems and policies. Participation in these groups empowers you personally and contributes to broader changes that benefit all patients. By joining forces with similar experiences and challenges, you help build a more informed, empowered, and patient-centric healthcare system.

As this chapter closes, we reflect on the crucial role of patient advocacy groups in transforming individual patient experiences into powerful collective actions that shape better healthcare practices and policies. Looking ahead, the next chapter will explore the digital dimensions of patient care, focusing on how technological advancements are reshaping patient engagement and healthcare delivery. This discussion will delve into the evolving landscape of telehealth, electronic health records, and digital health tools, continuing our journey toward understanding and navigating the modern healthcare environment.

Chapter 14 The Digital Patient: Navigating Online Healthcare Resources

Imagine finding yourself in a situation where a sudden ailment or a routine check-up requires a doctor's consultation. However, stepping out of your home is not an option—perhaps due to a busy schedule, mobility issues, or even global health concerns such as a pandemic. Here, the marvel of modern medicine meets digital innovation in the form of telehealth, a dynamic and rapidly evolving field that transforms your living room into a virtual doctor's office. This shift redefines convenience and expands access to healthcare services, making medical consultation possible with just a few clicks. As we explore the realms of telehealth, you will discover how this modern healthcare solution fits and enhances your medical care experience, ensuring that you remain at the forefront of managing your health effectively.

14.1 Telehealth: The Future of Patient-Doctor Interaction

Telehealth has surged to the forefront of healthcare delivery, offering numerous benefits that address both logistical and medical challenges. Its convenience is unmatched; it allows you to receive healthcare services from the comfort of your home, eliminating travel time and reducing the disruption to your daily schedule. For those living in remote or underserved areas, telehealth is a critical link to essential healthcare services, ensuring that geographical location no longer dictates the quality of care one can access.

Moreover, telehealth appointments can often be scheduled with greater flexibility, accommodating your lifestyle better than traditional in-person visits. This flexibility is particularly beneficial for managing chronic conditions that require frequent monitoring, allowing for regular touchpoints with healthcare providers without the repeated inconvenience of office visits. The efficiency of telehealth is not just in managing ongoing health issues but also in its preventive care potential—regular virtual interactions with healthcare providers can lead to early diagnosis and management of health issues, potentially reducing the need for more complex treatments.

Preparing for a Telehealth Appointment

Preparation is critical to maximizing the benefits of a telehealth appointment. Start by ensuring you have a stable internet connection and a device capable of video conferencing. Test your equipment beforehand to avoid technical issues during the appointment. Prepare a list of symptoms, relevant medical history, and your questions for your healthcare provider. Just as you might bring a physical folder to an in-person visit, have any relevant documents or previous test results available to reference or show during your virtual visit.

It's also important to consider the setting for your appointment. Choose a quiet, private area to ensure you can speak freely about personal health details. Good lighting is important so your healthcare provider can see you clearly, which is especially crucial if they need to assess any physical symptoms visually.

Privacy and Security Considerations

While telehealth offers convenience and accessibility, it also necessitates careful consideration of privacy and security. To protect your personal health information, it's vital to use secure, encrypted platforms recommended by your healthcare provider. Be wary of using public Wi-Fi networks for telehealth sessions, as they can be more susceptible to security breaches. Ensure that the privacy policies of the telehealth platform are transparent and robust, reassuring you that your data is handled securely.

Maximizing Telehealth Benefits

Clear communication with your healthcare provider is essential to fully benefiting from telehealth. Be candid about your symptoms and concerns. If you have a monitoring device at home, such as a blood pressure cuff or a blood glucose monitor, share those readings with your provider during the appointment. This data can provide valuable insights into your health and help guide the discussion.

Deciding when to opt for telehealth over in-person visits can also affect your care. Telehealth is ideal for routine consultations, mental health sessions, and minor illnesses. However, it's important to recognize situations where in-person care is preferable, such as emergencies or detailed physical examinations. Understanding these parameters will help you make informed decisions about best using telehealth services alongside traditional healthcare methods.

Engaging in telehealth not only empowers you with greater control over your health management but also aligns with modern healthcare practices, ensuring you receive timely care in a manner that best suits your lifestyle. As you integrate telehealth into your regular healthcare routine, you'll find it an indispensable tool in your ongoing journey to maintain and improve your health.

14.2 Evaluating Health Information Online: Separating Fact from Fiction

In an era where information is just a click away, the digital landscape becomes both a tool and a challenge, especially when it comes to health information. The ability to discern credible health information from misleading content online is not just useful; it's crucial for managing your health effectively. Navigating this vast sea of information requires a sharp eye for detail and an understanding of a reliable source. Consider the scenario where you are searching online for information about managing diabetes. You will likely encounter a mix of expert advice, personal anecdotes, promotional content, and potentially harmful misinformation. To navigate this, start by assessing the credibility of the sources you encounter.

When evaluating online health information, the first step is to look at the source. Trustworthy sources are typically associated with known medical institutions, government health agencies, or reputable health organizations. These sources often provide evidence-based information that is peer-reviewed or clearly cited, ensuring that the information is not only current but also scientifically validated. For instance, if you're reading about new diabetes treatments, articles hosted on domains such as .edu (educational institutions), .gov (government websites), or established health organization websites are more likely to offer reliable information.

Furthermore, the credibility of online health content can also be gauged by examining the author's credentials and the article's publication date. Medical professionals, researchers, and specialists who write these articles often have their qualifications listed. This transparency allows you to verify their expertise in the subject matter. Also, health information changes rapidly, so ensuring the content is up-to-date is essential. Information that is several years old may need to be more accurate or could have been superseded by new research.

Navigating the pitfalls of misinformation online entails a proactive approach—always cross-reference information. If you read about a new treatment or a health tip, check if this information is consistent across multiple reputable sites. This practice helps validate the accuracy of the information and protects you from acting on potentially harmful advice. Misinformation often spreads faster than factual information, especially if it sounds sensational or promises quick fixes. Being skeptical of such claims and verifying them through cross-referencing can shield you from the risks associated with misinformation.

Recommended Health Websites

To aid in your quest for accurate health information, here are several recommended websites known for their reliable content:

1. **Centers for Disease Control and Prevention (CDC)** - Offers comprehensive information on various health conditions, public health programs, and safety guidelines.
2. **World Health Organization (WHO)** - Provides global health updates, research findings, and international health standards.
3. **Mayo Clinic** - Known for detailed articles on diseases, symptoms, and treatments, all reviewed by medical experts.
4. **National Institutes of Health (NIH)** - Features extensive research-based information on a wide array of health topics and ongoing medical trials.
5. **MedlinePlus** - A service of the NIH, providing information on health conditions, drugs, and supplements, including a medical encyclopedia.

By utilizing these resources, you ensure access to information that is accurate, comprehensive, and vetted by healthcare professionals.

Developing critical thinking skills is essential when navigating online health information. Start by questioning the motives behind the information presented. Ask yourself: Is the article trying to sell something? Does it provide evidence for its claims? Is it exaggerating the truth to create sensationalism? Being critical and questioning the content and intent behind the information can significantly enhance your ability to discern factual information from fiction.

Moreover, consider the quality of evidence supporting the health claims. Reliable information is typically backed by scientific research, often cited directly in the article. Understanding how to look for and evaluate this evidence plays a crucial part in verifying the credibility of health information. This process involves recognizing the difference between anecdotal evidence and studies conducted under rigorous scientific conditions. For example, personal testimonials about a new drug's effectiveness are less reliable than results published in a peer-reviewed medical journal describing controlled clinical trials.

14.3 Leveraging Social Media for Health Advocacy

In today's interconnected world, social media platforms have transcended their original purpose of connectivity and entertainment, evolving into powerful tools for health advocacy. This transformation offers individuals like you an unprecedented opportunity to amplify your voice on health issues that matter deeply to you and your community. However, utilizing social media for health advocacy requires a responsible approach to ensure that your efforts are effective and ethical and contribute positively to public discourse on health.

Using social media responsibly begins with conscious sharing. When you decide to share personal stories or health information, it's crucial to consider your content's accuracy and impact. Personal stories can humanize complex health issues and inspire action, but they must be shared with sensitivity to privacy and respect for the experiences of others. Before posting, reflect on the purpose of your share: Is it to educate, advocate, or inspire? Is the information accurate and supported by credible sources? This mindfulness ensures that your contributions enhance understanding and support advocacy goals without inadvertently spreading misinformation.

Moreover, the tone and language used in social media posts significantly influence their reception. Strive for a tone that is inclusive and respectful, avoiding sensationalism. This approach not only fosters constructive dialogue but also builds trust and credibility with your audience. It's equally important to respect the privacy of others by not sharing information about someone else's health without their explicit consent. These practices ensure that your social media use aligns with broader ethical standards and respects the rights and dignity of all individuals.

In building online communities focused on specific health conditions or advocacy efforts, the goal is to create supportive, informative, and empowering spaces. Start by identifying platforms that best suit your advocacy goals—whether it's a Facebook group, a Twitter chat, or a LinkedIn network. Each platform has unique features and audiences, making some more suitable than others for different types of engagement. For instance, Instagram might be ideal for sharing compelling visual content related to mental health awareness, while LinkedIn could be more appropriate for professional discussions on healthcare policy.

Once you choose a platform, engage actively and constructively. Post regularly, respond to comments, and participate in discussions to keep the community vibrant and engaged. Encourage members to share their experiences and insights, fostering a collaborative environment where all voices are heard and valued. It's also beneficial to establish clear guidelines for interactions within your community to maintain a respectful and supportive atmosphere.

Navigating the risks of sharing personal health information on social media is critical. Privacy concerns are paramount, as information shared online can often be accessed by unintended audiences, including insurance companies, employers, and hackers. To protect your privacy, customize your privacy settings to control who can see your posts. Be cautious about sharing sensitive personal health information, and consider the long-term implications of publicizing such details.

Misinformation is another significant risk. The viral nature of social media can quickly spread inaccurate health information, leading to confusion and potentially harmful behaviors. Combat this by fact-checking content before sharing and providing sources for your health information. Encourage your community members to do the same, cultivating an environment where accuracy is valued over sensationalism.

Amplifying your voice through social media involves more than just broadcasting messages; it requires meaningful engagement with others. Connect with healthcare professionals, organizations, and policymakers who can help drive change. Use hashtags to increase the visibility of your posts, participate in relevant online events, and collaborate with influencers who share your commitment to health advocacy. By strategically engaging with a broader network, you can extend your reach and impact, bringing greater attention to the issues you care about.

In leveraging social media for health advocacy, you harness the power of digital connectivity to foster change, educate others, and advocate for better health outcomes. By approaching this tool with responsibility, strategic engagement, and a commitment to ethical standards, your efforts can significantly shape a healthier future for all.

16

Chapter 15 The Intersection of Healthcare and Technology

Imagine waking up each morning with the power to predict and manage your health as seamlessly as you check your email. The advent of wearable technology has revolutionized how we interact with the world and monitor and manage our health. This fusion of healthcare and technology is not just about convenience; it's about empowering you with real-time data to make informed decisions about your health and lifestyle.

15.1 Wearable Technology: A New Era of Personal Health Monitoring

Overview of Wearable Technology

Wearable health technology, encompassing devices like fitness trackers, smartwatches, and health monitors, has seamlessly integrated into our daily lives. These devices have sensors that track various health metrics such as heart rate, sleep patterns, activity levels, and even blood oxygen saturation. Some more advanced wearables offer electrocardiogram (ECG) monitoring and stress tracking, providing insights that were once only available in clinical settings.

Thanks to advancements in sensor technology and machine learning algorithms, these devices' capabilities continue to expand. They can now offer personalized insights by analyzing the accumulated data to detect abnormal patterns and potential health issues. For instance, some devices can alert you to an irregular heartbeat, potentially indicating cardiac issues that warrant further medical investigation. This proactive approach to health monitoring is a paradigm shift from reactive healthcare, where treatment begins only after symptoms appear and diagnoses are made.

Benefits of Personal Health Monitoring

The benefits of using wearable technology for personal health monitoring are manifold. Firstly, these devices promote an active lifestyle by tracking physical activity and providing motivational feedback. Many users find that having real-time data about their daily activity levels encourages them to move more and achieve their fitness goals. This is particularly beneficial in combating sedentary lifestyles, which are linked to numerous health issues such as obesity, type 2 diabetes, and cardiovascular diseases.

Moreover, for individuals managing chronic conditions such as hypertension or diabetes, wearables can be instrumental in tracking crucial parameters like blood pressure and blood glucose levels. This continuous monitoring helps maintain lifestyle adjustments and medication adherence to managing these conditions effectively. The immediacy of data allows for timely interventions, potentially preventing emergencies and improving overall health outcomes.

Data Privacy and Security

However, the increasing sophistication of wearable technologies also raises significant concerns about data privacy and security. The personal health information collected by these devices is highly sensitive and could lead to privacy violations and even identity theft if accessed by unauthorized parties. Therefore, it is imperative to ensure that your devices and apps comply with health data regulations, such as those in the U.S. The Health Insurance Portability and Accountability Act (HIPAA) sets the standard for protecting sensitive patient data.

To safeguard your information, opt for devices and services that encrypt data both in transit and at rest. Be wary of devices that store large amounts of personal data without adequate security measures. Regularly updating your devices and applications can also protect against security vulnerabilities. Moreover, be cautious about the permissions you grant to applications associated with your devices; ensure they only have access to the data they need to function correctly.

Integrating Data with Healthcare Providers

The potential for integrating data from wearable technology

with healthcare providers presents a transformative opportunity in medical care. By sharing your health data with your healthcare team, you can enable a more holistic view of your health outside the clinical environment. This integration can enhance the personalization of your care, allowing healthcare providers to tailor treatments and advice based on your real-world health data.

For instance, data from a fitness tracker could help a cardiologist better understand a patient's exercise tolerance and recovery heart rate, which are crucial for managing heart conditions. Similarly, sleep pattern data can be invaluable to a specialist treating sleep disorders. The key to effective integration lies in the interoperability of healthcare systems and wearable technologies, which must communicate seamlessly to ensure that the data shared is accurate, timely, and secure.

This integration also demands a collaborative approach to healthcare, where patients and providers work together to interpret and act on the data. It emphasizes the shift towards preventive healthcare, where the goal is to treat illness and maintain wellness.

In embracing wearable technology, you are equipped with tools that monitor your health and provide insights that empower you to live a healthier life. As we continue to explore the intersection of healthcare and technology, the potential to enhance patient care and treatment outcomes is boundless, promising a future where technology and personal health are inextricably linked.

15.2 Personalized Medicine: Tailoring Treatment to Your Genetic Blueprint

The concept of personalized medicine is a transformative approach in modern healthcare, fundamentally altering how treatments are developed and administered. At its core, personalized medicine utilizes your unique genetic and genomic information to tailor medical treatments as individual as you are. This bespoke approach improves the effectiveness of treatments and significantly reduces the risk of adverse reactions, setting a new standard in healthcare precision.

Principles of Personalized Medicine

Personalized medicine, often also referred to as precision medicine, hinges on the understanding that each individual's genetic makeup is unique. This uniqueness can affect how you respond to different medications and treatments. By analyzing genetic markers, doctors can predict the likelihood of disease occurrence, anticipate its progression, and tailor preventive or therapeutic interventions that are specifically effective for you. This method contrasts sharply with the traditional 'one-size-fits-all' approach, where treatments and dosages are standardized for the average person but may only work optimally for some.

Genetic information is gathered through various forms of testing, which identify specific biomarkers crucial in understanding how certain diseases manifest in your body. For instance, the presence of certain genetic markers might indicate a higher risk of developing conditions like breast cancer or cardiovascular diseases. Knowing this, your healthcare provider can suggest lifestyle changes or preventive measures long before symptoms appear, potentially saving your life or significantly improving its quality.

Advancements in Genetic Testing

The field of genetic testing has seen rapid advancements in recent years, significantly enhancing the scope and accuracy of personalized medicine. Techniques such as whole-genome sequencing and single-nucleotide polymorphism (SNP) analysis allow detailed insights into your genetic endowment. These advancements have made it possible to look for known markers associated with specific conditions and discover new genetic variations that may influence health.

These genetic tests are becoming faster, more accurate, and considerably less expensive, making them more accessible to a broader population. Such accessibility is crucial in integrating personalized medicine into everyday healthcare. For example, pharmacogenomics, a sub-field of personalized medicine, involves testing how your genes affect your body's response to drugs. This is particularly important in choosing the right medication and dosage for treatments involving pain management, psychological disorders, and chronic diseases, thereby reducing trial and error and minimizing side effects.

Considerations and Challenges

However, the shift towards personalized medicine has its challenges. Ethical issues, particularly concerning genetic privacy and data handling, are at the forefront of debates. There is a delicate balance between using genetic data to improve health outcomes and protecting that data from misuse. Genetic information is incredibly personal and, in the wrong hands, could lead to genetic discrimination in areas like employment and insurance.

Accessibility remains another significant challenge. While costs are decreasing, genetic testing and personalized treatments can still be expensive and not universally covered by insurance. There is also the issue of healthcare disparity; individuals in lower socio-economic groups or developing countries might find it harder to access these advanced medical solutions, potentially widening the gap in health equity.

Moreover, interpreting genetic information requires highly specialized knowledge. The medical community continues to grapple with the best ways to integrate and analyze this data comprehensively. Misinterpretations can lead to incorrect conclusions about an individual's health risks, demonstrating the need for ongoing education and training in genetic literacy for healthcare providers.

Future of Personalized Medicine

Looking ahead, personalized medicine has immense potential to revolutionize healthcare. Innovations in gene editing technologies, like CRISPR, promise to treat and potentially cure genetic disorders by correcting mutations at the DNA level. As research progresses, we anticipate more sophisticated methods of integrating genomic data with environmental and lifestyle factors, providing a holistic approach to health management.

The convergence of bioinformatics, genomics, and artificial intelligence is set to enhance personalized medicine's predictive power further. These technologies can help analyze vast amounts of genetic data more swiftly and accurately, predict disease risks, and personalize health interventions. As we unravel the human genome and understand its complexities, the promise of treatments tailored to individual genetic profiles is becoming a reality, heralding a new era in medical care where treatments are not just based on symptoms but rooted in a profound understanding of personal biology.

15.3 Protecting Your Health Data: Privacy in the Digital Age

In an era where our most intimate details are potentially just a click away from public exposure, health data privacy emerges as a paramount concern. Every day, vast amounts of personal health information are exchanged across networks, stored on servers, and analyzed by algorithms. This digital revolution in healthcare brings immense benefits by enabling better disease tracking, enhancing patient care, and facilitating medical research. However, it also introduces significant risks, notably the threats of data breaches and unauthorized access, which could lead to identity theft, discrimination, and even manipulation of health data.

Health data's sensitivity makes it a prime target for cyberattacks.

Hospitals, insurance companies, and other healthcare providers store comprehensive personal health records, including medical history and genetic information. A breach of such data not only undermines your privacy but also exposes you to risks ranging from blackmail to health insurance fraud. Furthermore, as the connectivity between medical devices and health systems increases, so does the potential for hackers to exploit vulnerabilities in less secure systems, potentially leading to catastrophic results.

To navigate these waters safely, understanding your health data rights is crucial. Under laws like the Health Insurance Portability and Accountability Act (HIPAA) in the United States, you have the right to access your medical records, request corrections to your health information, and obtain a record of disclosures of your health data. These rights empower you to take control of your health information, ensuring that you are informed about what data is collected, how it is used, and who has access to it. However, the legal landscape can be complex, and the protections vary by country, highlighting the importance of familiarizing yourself with local regulations.

Best Practices for Data Protection

Protecting your health data starts with understanding where and how this information is stored and shared. Opt for healthcare providers and services that adhere to stringent data protection standards and have robust security measures in place. At a personal level, be cautious about sharing sensitive health information online or via apps. Always verify the security credentials of any digital health service, looking for encryption standards and security certifications that ensure your data is handled securely.

Furthermore, regular monitoring of your health accounts, much like you would with your bank accounts, can help you spot any unauthorized access or discrepancies early. Use strong, unique passwords for your health-related accounts, and consider using two-factor authentication for an added layer of security. Be wary of phishing scams and suspicious links attempting to steal sensitive information, and ensure your home network is secured with up-to-date antivirus software and firewalls.

Navigating Consent and Data Sharing

Consent forms the cornerstone of data sharing in healthcare. When you are asked to share your health data with healthcare providers, researchers, or apps, fully understanding what you consent to is vital. Read the terms and conditions carefully— know what data is being collected, how long it will be stored, and the purposes for which it will be used. If anything is unclear, do not hesitate to ask questions. You can limit how your health information is used or disclosed, particularly regarding secondary uses like marketing or research.

Data-sharing agreements should be transparent and based on an opt-in model, where you actively give your consent rather than having it assumed. Be particularly cautious about sharing genetic information, which has implications for your privacy and potentially for your family members. In cases where data sharing can lead to significant discoveries or enhancements in patient care, such as in research studies, weigh the benefits against the risks and make an informed decision that aligns with your values and privacy expectations.

As we continue integrating technology into our healthcare systems, vigilance in protecting our health data becomes more critical. By understanding your rights, implementing best practices for data protection, and navigating consent and data sharing with care, you empower yourself to protect your privacy and contribute to the broader integrity of our healthcare systems. This chapter serves as a guide, helping you to safeguard your most personal information as we step forward into an increasingly digital healthcare landscape.

As we close this chapter on the crucial topic of health data privacy, we focus on the broader implications of digital health technologies. The next chapter will explore how these technologies transform patient care and challenge us to rethink the ethics and impact of digital health. From telemedicine to AI in diagnostics, the digital revolution is reshaping the healthcare landscape, offering unprecedented opportunities and raising new ethical dilemmas. As we navigate this evolving terrain, staying informed and proactive about our digital health interactions ensures that we benefit from technological advancements and protect our fundamental rights and values in the healthcare domain.

Chapter 16 Envisioning a Patient-Centered Healthcare System

Imagine a healthcare landscape where your treatment is tailored not just to a statistically average patient but uniquely to you, incorporating your genetic profile, lifestyle, and even your preferences for delivering care. This vision isn't derived from a distant, utopian future; it's the emerging reality of patient-centered healthcare, empowered by innovations that promise to fundamentally transform how we interact with medical professionals, manage our health, and perceive the role of technology in medicine.

16.1 Beyond the Status Quo: Innovations That Could Transform Healthcare

Decentralized Health Models

In pursuing a more patient-centered healthcare system, de-centralized health models stand out for their revolutionary approach to enhancing patient autonomy and care accessibility. Unlike traditional centralized models, where decision-making and resource allocation are confined to a few significant players, decentralized healthcare systems distribute these elements across a more comprehensive network of care providers and stakeholders. This shift empowers patients by giving them more control over their health decisions and facilitates a more personalized healthcare experience.

By leveraging mobile health apps and telemedicine technologies, decentralized models break down geographical barriers, making healthcare accessible in remote areas where traditional services are scarce. For instance, a patient living in a rural area can receive consultations and ongoing care from specialists in a metropolitan center without the need for extensive travel. This model not only improves access but also ensures that healthcare delivery is more tailored to each patient's individual needs, respecting their time, preferences, and specific health conditions.

Digital Twins in Healthcare

The concept of digital twins—a cutting-edge innovation originally developed for industrial applications—has found promising potential in healthcare. In this context, a digital twin is a virtual representation of a patient's health profile created using real-time data from various medical and environmental sources. This comprehensive digital construct allows healthcare providers to simulate different treatment scenarios, predict outcomes, and make more informed decisions tailored to patients' unique health dynamics.

The implications for diagnosis, treatment, and preventive care are profound. For example, by analyzing the digital twin of a heart patient, doctors can predict potential complications or the likelihood of a drug's efficacy, thereby customizing treatments that optimize health outcomes while minimizing risks. This technology enhances the precision of healthcare and shifts the focus from reactive to proactive, anticipating health issues before they manifest physically.

Blockchain for Medical Records

Blockchain technology, best known for its role in cryptocurrencies, offers transformative potential for managing medical records with enhanced security, transparency, and interoperability. By creating decentralized and immutable ledgers of medical records, blockchain ensures that patient data is secure from tampering and readily available across different healthcare providers as needed.

The patient-controlled aspect of blockchain in healthcare stands to revolutionize patient privacy and data accessibility. Patients can have complete control over who accesses their medical information and under what circumstances, all facilitated through blockchain's secure, permission-based access. This protects privacy and empowers patients in their healthcare journeys, ensuring that their medical history is a facilitator, not a barrier, to receiving personalized care.

AI-driven Predictive Care

Artificial intelligence (AI) and machine learning are at the forefront of transforming healthcare into a predictive, rather than merely reactive, service. AI-driven predictive care utilizes algorithms and massive datasets to identify patterns that human providers might overlook. This includes predicting outbreaks of illnesses in populations and foreseeing individual health events before they occur, such as anticipating diabetic complications or heart failures.

By integrating AI into daily health management tools—like wearable devices that monitor heart rate, sleep patterns, and physical activity—patients and providers can gain insights that lead to early intervention. This early diagnostic capability can dramatically alter the course of treatment, shifting the emphasis to prevention and significantly improving patient outcomes while reducing the need for costly and invasive procedures.

These innovations, emblematic of a shift towards more dynamic, personalized, and patient-centered healthcare systems, promise to adapt to the specific needs of individuals and preemptively address health issues, revolutionizing our approach to health and wellness. As we continue to explore and integrate these technologies, the very fabric of healthcare as we know it is poised for transformation, marking a new era of medical treatment as unique as each patient it serves.

16.2 Building Bridges: Integrating Alternative and Conventional Medicine

In healthcare, the melding of alternative and conventional medicine forms a bridge between centuries-old practices and modern scientific approaches, creating a comprehensive treatment paradigm that respects diverse healing traditions grounded in robust evidence. When approached thoughtfully, this integration can significantly enhance patient care by providing multiple therapeutic options catering to individual needs and preferences.

Evidence-based Integration

The core of successfully combining alternative and conventional medicine lies in adhering to evidence-based practices. This approach involves rigorous evaluation of alternative therapies using scientific methods to establish their efficacy and safety. By doing so, healthcare providers can offer treatments that are not only culturally sensitive but also clinically effective. For instance, acupuncture, once considered purely an alternative therapy, has been shown through numerous studies to be effective in managing chronic pain and has subsequently been incorporated into conventional treatment plans. Similarly, mindfulness and meditation, validated by scientific research, are now recommended as part of treatment for various mental health conditions, including depression and anxiety. This evidence-based integration ensures that all treatment options, whether conventional or alternative, are held to the same standard of proof, guaranteeing that the best possible care is delivered to patients.

Patient Preferences and Values

Understanding and respecting patient preferences and values is paramount in the integrated healthcare model. Everyone comes with their beliefs, cultural backgrounds, and personal experiences that shape their health choices. In recognizing and valuing these individual aspects, healthcare providers can create a therapeutic alliance that fosters trust and improves health outcomes. For example, some patients may prefer herbal remedies over pharmaceutical medications due to cultural beliefs or past experiences. When these preferences are supported by evidence of efficacy and safety, integrating these choices into their care can enhance satisfaction and encourage greater compliance with treatment plans. Moreover, this respect for patient preferences underscores the patient-centered nature of modern healthcare, which prioritizes the individual's overall well-being over a one-size-fits-all approach.

Regulatory Framework

A robust regulatory framework is essential to ensure the safety and efficacy of integrated medical practices. This framework should oversee the licensing of alternative medicine practitioners and monitor the quality and sourcing of herbal medicines and other supplements. By establishing stringent regulatory standards akin to those applied to conventional medicine, patients can trust the treatments they receive, regardless of whether these are based on traditional knowledge or modern science. Furthermore, such regulation helps maintain professional standards among practitioners, ensuring that those who deliver alternative medical treatments have the qualifications and adhere to ethical practices. This regulatory oversight is crucial in protecting patients from potentially harmful treatments and ensuring that all health interventions contribute positively to their well-being.

Educational Initiatives

Education prepares healthcare professionals to operate effectively within an integrated healthcare model. Medical curricula must encompass conventional medical training and a thorough understanding of various alternative therapies. This education should focus on the mechanisms and benefits of different treatments and when and how to integrate them safely into patient care. Additionally, ongoing professional development courses and workshops can keep healthcare providers updated on the latest research and developments in both fields. These educational initiatives ensure that healthcare professionals are well-equipped to make informed decisions about integrating therapies and providing balanced and informed care options to their patients.

Integrating alternative and conventional medicine represents a progressive step towards a holistic healthcare system that honors human diversity in healing practices. It offers a more nuanced approach to treatment that respects patient preferences and is grounded in rigorous scientific validation. As we continue to build these bridges, we pave the way for a healthcare environment that not only heals but also deeply respects the cultural and personal contexts of each patient it serves.

18

Chapter 17 The Global Health Perspective

Imagine a world where an infectious disease outbreak in one country can be swiftly contained and catalyze strengthening healthcare systems globally. This isn't merely a romantic dream but a practical necessity underscored by recent global health crises. The lessons we've learned from pandemics are not just about survival; they are blueprints for building a more resilient, equitable, and interconnected global health infrastructure. As we delve into these lessons, remember that each insight contributes to a larger goal: a world where excellent healthcare transcends borders and is viewed as a shared global asset.

17.1 Lessons from Global Pandemics: Strengthening Healthcare Systems

Preparedness and Response

The onset of a pandemic brings challenges, from overwhelming healthcare facilities to rapidly depleting resources, revealing the cracks in even the most robust health systems. However, through these challenges, we've gleaned invaluable lessons on preparedness and response that emphasize the importance of global cooperation. For instance, the COVID-19 pandemic highlighted the critical need for real-time data sharing and international collaboration in disease surveillance and response.

Countries that had invested in pandemic preparedness, like South Korea and New Zealand, could implement effective testing and contact tracing systems rapidly. These actions were supported by a framework of international cooperation that facilitated sharing of information and resources. The lesson here is clear: global pandemics require global responses. By strengthening international health regulations and cooperation frameworks, such as those coordinated by the World Health Organization, we can enhance our collective ability to respond to health emergencies more effectively.

Health Equity and Access

Global pandemics disproportionately affect populations in low-resource settings, often exacerbating existing health inequities. However, these crises also provide an opportunity to redesign our global health approach, emphasizing equity and access more strongly. For instance, initiatives like COVAX aim to ensure equitable access to COVID-19 vaccines by pooling resources to support vaccine procurement and distribution in lower-income countries.

This approach not only addresses the immediate needs of the pandemic but also sets a precedent for tackling other global health challenges, such as HIV/AIDS and tuberculosis, which continue to disproportionately burden low-resource settings. Promoting health equity on a global scale involves more than just emergency responses; it requires a sustained commitment to strengthening healthcare systems, improving access to healthcare services, and addressing social determinants of health that contribute to disparities.

Technology and Innovation Transfer

The transfer of technology and innovation across borders has proven to be a cornerstone of strengthening healthcare systems globally. During the COVID-19 pandemic, the rapid development and dissemination of diagnostic tools and technologies showcased how crucial technological adaptability is to health system resilience.

Countries that could quickly adapt and deploy new technologies, such as mobile apps for contact tracing or platforms for telemedicine consultations, demonstrated greater agility in managing the pandemic's impact. This adaptability is about adopting foreign technologies and fostering an environment where innovations can be locally adapted and scaled. By sup-

porting technology transfer initiatives and facilitating collabo-
rations between high-tech hubs and emerging economies, we
can ensure that innovations reach where they are most needed,
enhancing global health security.

Building Resilient Healthcare Infrastructure

Lastly, the resilience of healthcare infrastructure is the most
critical lesson from recent pandemics. Resilient systems can
withstand shocks from sudden surges in patient numbers or
disruptions in global supply chains. Building such resilience
requires a multifaceted approach, focusing on sustainability
and adaptability.

Investments in healthcare infrastructure must go beyond hospitals and clinics to include robust supply chains, reliable information systems, and flexible resource allocation mechanisms.
Moreover, the concept of 'surge capacity,' which includes protocols and resources in place to expand service capacity quickly, is
vital. Countries that integrated surge capacity into their health
systems were better equipped to handle the increases in patient
load during peak pandemic periods.

Incorporating these lessons into national and international
health planning can transform our global response to future
health crises, making our systems more responsive and robust.
By viewing global health through shared responsibility and
mutual benefit, we can build a future where health emergencies
prompt cooperation and innovation rather than chaos and
disparity.

19

Conclusion

As we draw the curtains on our journey through the healthcare industry's labyrinthine corridors, it is imperative to revisit and reflect on the pervasive issues that have shaped our discussions. From the overpowering influence of pharmaceutical companies to the convoluted insurance systems, the challenges in accessing care, and the ethical dilemmas that plague the system, we've uncovered the multifaceted problems that demand our attention and action.

But beyond the critical examination, this book has been a clarion call for empowerment and change. The critical takeaway is unmistakable: the empowerment of patients is non-negotiable. Health literacy, the potential of technological innovations, and advocating for transparency and ethical practices are not just optional extras but essential pillars upon which a reformed healthcare system must stand. A system where patient-centered care is the hallmark and every decision, policy, and practice is scrutinized through its impact on patient well-being.

Throughout these pages, we've encountered personal narratives and case studies that have illustrated the human cost of a faltering healthcare system and highlighted the indomitable spirit of individuals advocating for better care. These stories serve as both a warning and an inspiration, reminding us of what is at stake and the power of resilience and advocacy.

Envisioning a reformed healthcare system is not a utopian dream but a feasible reality if we prioritize patient well-being over profit, integrate evidence-based alternatives and conventional medicine, and leverage technology to tailor personalized care. This vision for the future is inclusive, innovative, and inspired by the very real needs of those it serves.

Now, the onus is on you, the reader. Please take up the mantle of advocacy for your own health and systemic change. Engage with policy discussions, support healthcare reforms, and contribute to a movement towards a more ethical and patient-focused system. Your voice is crucial in the chorus calling for change.

The path to healthcare reform is complex and requires the collaboration of all stakeholders—patients, healthcare professionals, policymakers, and the broader community. It is a collective effort that demands persistence, empathy, and a shared healthcare vision of equity and justice.

Let us remember the power of informed decision-making, advocacy, and collective action. Hope is on the horizon, fueled by our combined efforts to advocate for a system that truly serves the needs of all. Together, we can transform the healthcare landscape into one that upholds the principles of fairness, accessibility, and compassion. Let this book not just reflect what is but a beacon of what could be. Thank you for joining me on this vital journey. Let's continue striving for a healthcare system that we can all be proud of—one that cherishes and protects every life it touches.

20

References

- *The Dark Side of the Pharmaceutical Industry* https://www.aj
  mc.com/view/the-dark-side-of-the-pharmaceutical-indu
  stry

- *Americans' Challenges with Health Care Costs* https://www.kf
  f.org/other/issue-brief/americans-challenges-with-healt
  h-care-costs/

- *Lobbying Expenditures and Campaign Contributions by the ...*
  https://www.ncbi.nlm.nih.gov/pmc/articles/PMC7054854/

- *Alosetron: a case study in regulatory capture, or a victory ...*

https://www.ncbi.nlm.nih.gov/pmc/articles/PMC1124108/

- *Drug Policy 101: Pharmaceutical Marketing Tactics* https://ww
  w.kpihp.org/wp-content/uploads/2020/02/drug_policy_p
  harmaceutical_marketing_101_FINAL.pdf

- *Relationships between physicians and Pharma - PMC* https://w
  ww.ncbi.nlm.nih.gov/pmc/articles/PMC5765617/

- *Summary - Challenges for the FDA - NCBI Bookshelf* https://w
  ww.ncbi.nlm.nih.gov/books/NBK52919/#:~:text=The%20c
  ommittee%20identified%20four%20major,quality%20of
  %20postmarket%20data%20and

- *Health Care Privacy and Conflict-of-Interest Regulations ...*
  https://www.ncbi.nlm.nih.gov/books/NBK25561/

- *Data fraud in clinical trials - PMC* https://www.ncbi.nlm.nih.
  gov/pmc/articles/PMC4340084/

REFERENCES

- *Impact of Pharmacy Benefit Managers* https://www.common
  wealthfund.org/publications/explainer/2019/apr/pharmac
  y-benefit-managers-and-their-role-drug-spending

- *Patent cliff and strategic switch: exploring ...* https://www.ncb
  i.nlm.nih.gov/pmc/articles/PMC4899342/

- *Are Pharmaceutical Patents Protected By Human Rights?*
  https://www.ncbi.nlm.nih.gov/pmc/articles/PMC4704437/

- *What Is Patient Experience?* https://www.ahrq.gov/cahps/ab
  out-cahps/patient-experience/index.html

- *Challenges in personalized management of chronic ...* https://w
  ww.ncbi.nlm.nih.gov/pmc/articles/PMC4765020/

- *The Burden of Medical Debt in the United States* https://www.
  kff.org/health-costs/issue-brief/the-burden-of-medical-
  debt-in-the-united-states/
- *Rural Health Disparities Overview* https://www.ruralhealthin
  fo.org/topics/rural-health-disparities

- *Food and Drug Administration Recalls - StatPearls* https://ww w.ncbi.nlm.nih.gov/books/NBK570589/

- *Adverse Drug Reactions - StatPearls - NCBI Bookshelf* https://w ww.ncbi.nlm.nih.gov/books/NBK599521/#:~:text=In%202 022%2C%20there%20were%20over,such%20visits%20su bsequently%20require%20hospitalization.

- *Long-Term Effects Of Psychotropic Drugs Are ... - NPR* https://w ww.npr.org/sections/health-shots/2018/02/27/589081018/ long-term-effects-of-psychotropic-drugs-are-cloaked-i n-mystery

- *Integrative Medicine: What Is It, Types, Risks & Benefits* https://my.clevelandclinic.org/health/treatments/2168 3-integrative-medicine

- *Glossary of Health Coverage and Medical Terms* https://www. cms.gov/CCIIO/Resources/Forms-Reports-and-Other-Res ources/Downloads/uniform-glossary-final.pdf

- *How to appeal an insurance company decision* https://www.h ealthcare.gov/appeal-insurance-company-decision/

- *The Evolution of the Telehealth Appointment and Its Impact on Modern Healthcare* https://www.decent.com/blog/the-evol ution-of-the-telehealth-appointment-and-its-impact-o n-modern-healthcare#:~:text=It%20brings%20unparalle led%20convenience%20and,underserved%20areas%20wit h%20video%20visits.

- *Digital Health Literacy | PSNet - AHRQ* https://psnet.ahrq.go v/primer/digital-health-literacy#:~:text=Digital%20healt h%20literacy%20is%20positively,literacy%20and%20acc ess%20to%20technology.&text=Higher%20levels%20of% 20digital%20health,in%20managing%20chronic%20healt h%20conditions.

- *Comparisons of Health Care Systems in the United States, ...* https://www.ncbi.nlm.nih.gov/pmc/articles/PMC3633404/

- *The Pros and Cons of Single-Payer Health Plans* https://www. urban.org/sites/default/files/publication/99918/pros_and _cons_of_a_single-payer_plan.pdf

- *What Is Direct Primary Care, and What Are Its Benefits?* https://www.goodrx.com/hcp/students/direct-primary -care

- *Transforming Health Care from the Ground Up* https://hbr.org/ 2018/07/transforming-health-care-from-the-ground-up

- *An Update on the Application of CRISPR Technology ... - NCBI* https://www.ncbi.nlm.nih.gov/pmc/articles/PMC10239226 /#:~:text=CRISPR%2Dbased%20therapies%20are%20curr ently,PD%2D1%20altered%20T%20cells.

- *AI in healthcare: A double-edged sword? Study reveals impact ...* https://www.news-medical.net/news/20231219/AI-in-h ealthcare-A-double-edged-sword-Study-reveals-impact- on-diagnostic-accuracy.aspx

- *Blockchain technology in healthcare: A systematic review* https://www.ncbi.nlm.nih.gov/pmc/articles/PMC9000089/

- *The 5 Most Pressing Ethical Issues in Biotech Medicine* https://w

ww.ncbi.nlm.nih.gov/pmc/articles/PMC3570985/

· *Health Care Reform and Social Movements in the United ...* https://www.ncbi.nlm.nih.gov/pmc/articles/PMC2518596/

· *Health Advocacy: A Case Study* https://interprofessional.umi ch.edu/2018/03/29/health-advocacy-a-case-study/

· *Healthcare Management Ethics - A Positive View of Lobbying* https://www.chausa.org/publications/health-progress/arc hive/article/november-1993/healthcare-management-eth ics—-a-positive-view-of-lobbying

· *Using narratives to impact health policy-making: a systematic ...* https://health-policy-systems.biomedcentral.com/articl es/10.1186/s12961-019-0423-4

· *Prescription Drug Use and Misuse in the United States* https://w ww.samhsa.gov/data/sites/default/files/NSDUH-FFR2-201 5/NSDUH-FFR2-2015.htm

· *Does long-term use of psychiatric drugs cause more harm ...* https://www.ncbi.nlm.nih.gov/pmc/articles/PMC4707562/

· *Effects of Mindfulness on Psychological Health: A Review ...* https://www.ncbi.nlm.nih.gov/pmc/articles/PMC3679190/

· *Exploring Barriers to Mental Health Care in the U.S.* https://www.aamcresearchinstitute.org/our-work/issue-brief/exploring-barriers-mental-health-care-us

· *Women's involvement in clinical trials: historical perspective ...* https://www.ncbi.nlm.nih.gov/pmc/articles/PMC4800017/

· *Gender bias in healthcare: Examples and consequences* https://www.medicalnewstoday.com/articles/gender-bias-in-healthcare

· *Beyond the Numbers: Access to Reproductive Health Care for Low-Income Women in Five Communities* https://www.kff.org/report-section/beyond-the-numbers-access-to-reproductive-health-care-for-low-income-women-in-five-co mmunities-executive-summary/

- *Advancing innovations in women's health through policy advo-cacy* https://www.path.org/our-impact/articles/advancing-innovations-in-womens-health-through-policy-advocac y/

- *Prescription opioid companies increased marketing after Purdue Pharma lawsuit, UW study shows* https://www.washington.e du/news/2023/10/09/prescription-opioid-companies-incr eased-marketing-after-purdue-pharma-lawsuit-uw-stu dy-shows/

- *How FDA Failures Contributed to the Opioid Crisis* https://pub med.ncbi.nlm.nih.gov/32880367/

- *Global Opioid Settlement | Office of the Attorney General* https://www.texasattorneygeneral.gov/globalopioidset tlement

- *Safely and Effectively Managing Pain Without Opioids* https://w

ww.cdc.gov/drugoverdose/featured-topics/pain-managem
ent.html

- *Patient Rights and Ethics – StatPearls* https://www.ncbi.nlm.
  nih.gov/books/NBK538279/

- *The Ultimate Guide To Disputing A Medical Bill And ...* https://t
  hecollegeinvestor.com/21732/disputing-medical-bill/

- *Patient Advocacy Organizations: Institutional Conflicts ... – NCBI*
  https://www.ncbi.nlm.nih.gov/pmc/articles/PMC4107906/

- *Summary of the HIPAA Privacy Rule* https://www.hhs.gov/hip
  aa/for-professionals/privacy/laws-regulations/index.html

- *Telehealth Benefits and Barriers – PMC* https://www.ncbi.nl
  m.nih.gov/pmc/articles/PMC7577680/

- *Evaluating Health Information* https://medlineplus.gov/eval

uatinghealthinformation.html

• *Risks and benefits of sharing patient information on social media* https://academic.oup.com/ehjdh/advance-article/doi/10.1093/ehjdh/ztae009/7606717

• *Telehealth Best Practices: A Comprehensive Guide* https://www.selecthub.com/telemedicine/telehealth-best-practices/

• *Top 10 Medical Wearables Trends in 2023* https://www.startus-insights.com/innovators-guide/medical-wearables-trends/

• *Ethical, legal, and social implications of incorporating personalized medicine into healthcare* https://www.ncbi.nlm.nih.gov/pmc/articles/PMC4296905/

• *A Guide to the Personal Health Information Protection Act* https://www.ipc.on.ca/wp-content/uploads/Resources/hguide-e.pdf

- *Challenges and recommendations for wearable devices in ...* https://www.ncbi.nlm.nih.gov/pmc/articles/PMC9931360/

- *Decentralization versus centralized governance of health services* https://www.ncbi.nlm.nih.gov/pmc/articles/PMC6752685/

- *Digital twins for health: a scoping review | npj Digital Medicine* https://www.nature.com/articles/s41746-024-01073-0

- *Blockchain Technology for Electronic Health Records - PMC* https://www.ncbi.nlm.nih.gov/pmc/articles/PMC9739765/

- *Integrating complementary and alternative medicine into ...* https://pubmed.ncbi.nlm.nih.gov/24885066/

- *Recommendations - Pandemic Preparedness | Lessons ...* https://www.cfr.org/report/pandemic-preparedness-lessons-COVID-19/recommendations/

- *Health equity: challenges in low-income countries - PMC* https://www.ncbi.nlm.nih.gov/pmc/articles/PMC2877288/

- *Health technology transfer - PMC* https://www.ncbi.nlm.nih.gov/pmc/articles/PMC1118623/

- *Building Health Care Sector Resilience* https://toolkit.climate.gov/topics/human-health/building-climate-resilience-health-sector

- *Lobbying Expenditures and Campaign Contributions by ...* https://www.ncbi.nlm.nih.gov/pmc/articles/PMC7054854/

- *Health Care System Reforms in Developing Countries - PMC* https://www.ncbi.nlm.nih.gov/pmc/articles/PMC4140377/

- *Role of civil society in health care: Mechanisms for realizing ...* https://www.frontiersin.org/journals/public-health/articles/10.3389/fpubh.2023.1091533/full

- *Health Care Reform and Social Movements in the United ...*
  https://www.ncbi.nlm.nih.gov/pmc/articles/PMC2518596/

About the Author

LaDonna Naturale is a certified holistic practitioner and a passionate advocate for a healthier, more sustainable, and non-toxic lifestyle. With over 25 years of experience in healthcare, LaDonna combines her professional expertise with a decade-long commitment to clean living. She shares practical tips and insights on home and product detoxification, empowering families to lead healthier lives. Through her journey, LaDonna inspires others to embrace holistic wellness and make informed choices for a better, sustainable future.

You can connect with me on:
- ⊕ https://www.otispublishing.com
- 🐦 https://www.twitter.com/OtisPublishing
- f https://www.facebook.com/otis.publishing

Subscribe to my newsletter:
- ✉ https://www.otispublishing.com/contact

Also by LaDonna Naturale

Nature's Pharmacy: Foraging Food and Medicine for Wellbeing Unlock the untapped potential of the great outdoors: Master the art of responsible foraging and trans- form your wellbeing in just weeks, even if you've never identified a single plant before!

Embark on an unforgettable journey of discovery and wellness with the wonders of nature. Seize this chance to enhance your life and the environment.

Cleanse and Reclaim: Detoxify Your Home for a Healthier Life Unlock a healthier, toxin-free lifestyle by purifying your home and environment.

Detoxifying your home isn't just a temporary fix, it's a lifestyle that provides long-term health benefits for you and your family.

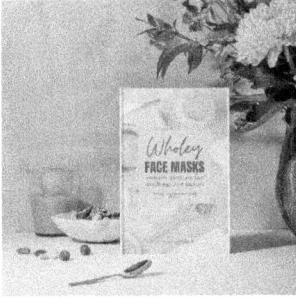

Wholey Face Masks: Holistic Skincare for Wellness and Beauty
Here's your invitation to a peaceful world of pure skin wellness and beauty, where you'll not just care for your skin but also connect with nature and, most importantly, yourself.

It's time to toss away the expensive, ineffective, and potentially harmful products that clutter your bathroom counter and embrace wholesome, natural skincare.

Embrace natural beauty, embark on a journey towards skin wellness, and have some fun along the way.

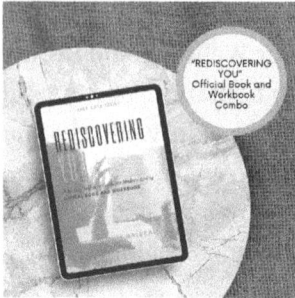

Rediscovering You: A Complete 30 Day Self-care Guide for Modern Living: OFFICIAL BOOK AND WORKBOOK

Begin your transformative journey of self-discovery and well-being with "Rediscovering You," a comprehensive 30-day self-care guide tailored to the demands of modern living.

This empowering book and workbook combo is designed to guide you through intentional and introspective practices, helping you reconnect with yourself in the midst of life's hustle.

As the foundation of my self-care series, this book and guided workbook, "Rediscovering You: A 30-Day Self-care Guide for Modern Living" book and workbook explains the importance of self-care and gives you practical ways to exercise self-care daily even in our busy modern-day lives.

www.ingramcontent.com/pod-product-compliance
Lightning Source LLC
Chambersburg PA
CBHW060224030426
42335CB00014B/1337